Living through Loss

"Where there is unimaginable suffering, growth and peace can be achieved. As Donna has shown us, turning to our heavenly Father can help pave the way. 'He heals the brokenhearted and binds up their wounds'" (Ps. 147:3 NIV).

—**KATHY A. GARCIA-LAWSON,** PhD, clinical psychologist

"It's every person's worst nightmare come true. . . . In a moment, Donna lost everything, or so it seemed. But she never lost hold of the One who was holding her. Donna takes us on her journey of healing, intimately sharing her pain and grief as she faced wave after wave of loss. Ultimately, this is a story of triumph over tragedy pointing to the all-sufficient love of a Savior who never leaves us in our darkest hour but carries us through the storms of life. Donna's story shows the redeeming, restorative, and loving heart of God."

—**VALINDA HUCK,** former women's ministry coordinator at Oak Hills Church Outer West, interpreter for the deaf at Oak Hills Church, San Antonio, Texas

"Donna has masterfully woven together the details of her story to make it completely relatable to all of us. We have all experienced loss. It is our responsibility to determine how we handle that loss. Donna's choice to follow our Lord and live for Him is an absolute inspiration. Her story has been one that I am eager to share with friends and strangers because it provides much-needed *hope* for broken hearts; it offers such hope at a time in history when many feel that hope no longer exists."

—**HEIDI CASTO,** MA, DDS, wife, mother, reading specialist, teacher, researcher

"My heart ached as I learned of Donna's devastating loss and her long and brave process of healing physically, emotionally, and spiritually. I was nodding my head page after page, remembering the roller coaster of emotions of becoming an instant widow back in 1999. Truly, God has given Donna this story to tell . . . for His glory and to give hope to many. Donna's story bolstered my faith and reminded me of how good our God is even in the worst of situations."

—DEBBIE CHRISTIAN, acquisitions editor, Bondfire Books

Living *through* Loss

THE
WAY
PRESS

Jupiter, Florida

THE WAY PRESS

Published by The Way Press
Donnamarieberger.com

This book is a memoir. It reflects the author's present recollections of experiences over time. Some names and characteristics have been changed, some events have been compressed, and some dialogue has been recreated.

Editing: Gail Fallen, gail@mesanetworks.net
Publishing and Design Services: MelindaMartin.me
Author Photo Credit: Jennifer J. Sampson
Cover Artwork: Magnolia Branch by Sandra+Mart/Shutterstock
     Seed Pod by marina+durante/Shutterstock

ISBN: 979-8-218-09036-4 (paperback); 978-1-0880-7480-0 (hardcover)

Living *through* Loss

a memoir of
RECOVERING JOY
after cumulative grief

Donna M Berger
with Will Searcy

THE
WAY
PRESS

Jupiter, Florida

To my husband, John,
who never left my side

To our children Christian, Meredith, and Laura,
you are a source of unending joy and support

To Gerry, Dawn, Stephen,
and Michael Michaud,
love is eternal

To all of you who are
missing a part of your heart today,
this book is for you

About the Cover

"In the fall of the year after the flowers are long gone from a magnolia tree, the seed pods have an interesting surprise in store. Magnolia seed pods spread open to reveal bright red berries, and the tree comes to life . . . Inside the berries, you'll find the magnolia seeds. And when conditions are just right, you may find a magnolia seedling growing under a magnolia tree."[1]

Because of its ability to adapt to different climates, the magnolia tree tends to live from eighty to one hundred years. For all these reasons, the magnolia tree has come to symbolize endurance and strength. These are two characteristics that *Living through Loss* highlights as essential to have or to develop on any journey through grief into healing.

Contents

Introduction

How do you go on living when someone you love with all your heart has been ripped from your grasp? Whom do you turn to when the one you always turn to is gone? How do you survive today when you wish with every breath you take to return to yesterday? These were just some of the questions that raced through my mind when my husband and our three young children were killed in a fiery car crash.

We all know someone who has lost a loved one, and most of us have been to a funeral and have heard a homily on loss, but absolutely nothing can prepare us for what we face when the one who dies is *our* child, *our* husband or wife, or *our* mom or dad or brother or sister. After the crash, I felt like I was walking a tightrope without a net. But, eventually, I made it to the other side, and I want to share how I was able to do that with you.

Grief is a combination of emotions and a natural response to loss. But grief is not a response limited to the loss of a loved one. We can find ourselves shrouded in grief from the loss of our dreams, opportunities, relationships, and even the loss of ourselves. And when that happens, we often blindly grasp at whatever is in reach. When I felt there was nowhere to turn, I turned to God, and my journey through grief became a spiritual journey into healing. You may be mad at God right now or feel that your pain is unbearable and that there is nothing that will take it away, but I promise you that if you take this walk with me, you will find comfort, peace, courage, and eventually joy again in your life. If you are grieving, sick, lonely, or oppressed, I invite you to read about how the Lord's faithfulness will restore your life as it has mine. I cannot do the very hard work of grieving for you, but I am here to let you know you are not alone. I wrote this book to share my life with you as a friend and companion and to guide you toward the light of hope hidden behind the dark clouds of despair.

Ideally, as you move from shock and denial to acceptance, you will find that the scars of a healed heart tell us where we have been but do not need to lead us to where we are going. When you finally reach that point of trust and sweet surrender to the Lord, He will bless you abundantly and you will have all that you need "in all things, at all times . . ." (2 Cor. 9:8 ESV). Jesus will be a light to your path, and you will once again experience joy in your life.

I pray you find the comfort and peace you seek through this story of God in my life, and I wish you Godspeed on your journey through grief into healing.

Love & Blessings,

Donna

Those who plant in tears will harvest with shouts of joy.
They weep as they go to plant their seed,
but they sing as they return with the harvest.

—PSALM 126:5–6 NLT

CHAPTER 1

The Seeds of Resilience

Faith was always a big part of my life, just not the faith I know today. The experiences of my life shared in this book taught me that I had to *"live by faith, not by sight."*

—2 CORINTHIANS 5:7 NIV

Perched atop a big brown suitcase, I nervously fingered the faux pearl buttons on my little pink sweater. Although my parents said I would be staying with my grandmother for "just a little while," an icy wave of fear coursed through my veins as the tug on my three-year-old heart whispered that something was wrong. My mom explained that I needed to keep my lonely grandmother company. This would be the first of many empty spaces in my heart.

I never understood. There were some twenty plus other grandchildren, but I was chosen because the family decided my mother, who was recovering from surgery, could not care for an active toddler in addition to my newborn brother, Michael. I felt abandoned, but the Lord, in His infinite wisdom, had the master plan in front of Him and would use this pain to prepare me for the hurricane that years later would blow into my life. I believe that God has woven *all* of my life's experiences into a cloak of strength and resilience for me. It is what I rely upon to be able to "Consider it pure joy . . . whenever [I] face trials of many kinds . . ." (James 1:2). The joy is not in the trial but in our growing closer to the Lord throughout our trials.

Just a little while became twelve years in my grandmother's cozy cottage on a tree-lined, dead-end street in Connecticut. Life in a large Italian family was in many ways a microcosm of the community. Several times a week, one of my five aunts would have "Mom," as we all called my grandmother, and me over for dinner, and I would get to play with my cousins. On Sundays after church, my six uncles and my half brother, Sonny, would come over with their children for a late morning snack of mom's freshly made meatballs, sausage, and eggplant carefully dusted with grated parmesan cheese, and I would have a whole different set of cousins as playmates. Afterward, Mom and I would usually drive to one of my aunt's or my parents' house for Sunday dinner. The food was always amazing, and there were usually two or three families gathered together, which provided a large enough group of cousins to form two teams for whichever games we decided to play.

My mother did not take her turn to host Mom and me as often as my aunts, so I didn't see my parents and brother on a weekly basis. It was a painful reminder at the end of those days when I said goodbye to my cousins and went back to my solitary existence with Mom. Then I'd dream about the world outside of the "family" and the dance lessons, swimming lessons, summer camps, and family vacations that I heard plenty about from my cousins.

For the most part, my childhood years were uneventful. I spent endless hours trying to catch fish in the river behind my grandmother's little house where I learned firsthand about ecosystems—small snakes, crayfish, and water bugs all dancing together in the harmony of predator and prey, of birth and death. I also enjoyed working in the dirt with Mom, who was an avid gardener. Everything was planted from seed, and the vegetables she produced were reminiscent of the bountiful Thanksgiving harvests. Besides vegetables, Mom's garden was a riot of color with dozens of annuals and perennials. She particularly loved her yellow rosebush, which never failed to bear the most fragrant and lovely blossoms year after year.

Unfortunately, much like that rosebush, living with Mom came with its share of thorns. She was very strict. Her husband died when her youngest was five years old and the oldest was nineteen. She was left alone to raise twelve children while dealing with the grief and loneliness of losing her life partner. Mom really did love me, but she was short-tempered, and I always needed to be on guard with this smart, creative woman who would fly into a rage at the smallest misstep.

One time, I was playing outside with my only doll. When I did not come in for dinner the minute she called, my grandmother ripped the doll out of my hands and threw it in the river.

Life was not all bad with Mom though. She was caring in her own way and very devout. We never missed Mass, the spring and fall novenas, the May Crowning, or any other church-related event. Mom said the Rosary every night and reminded me to pray as well. In retrospect, she had a "head relationship" with God, yet the times she lost her temper caused me to wonder if her heart was in it. Still, my faith journey began with Mom and the religious devotion she modeled for me.

Mom was an intelligent woman, and she put a great deal of emphasis on education. Each night, she would go over every aspect of my homework to make sure that it was correctly completed and that I was prepared for any tests or quizzes. She sent me to a Catholic school with four of my cousins, who made up the majority of my friends.

Once, when I was about seven years old, I was lucky enough to accompany my aunts and cousins to the beach. My cousins were older, and all knew how to swim, but under the strict guardianship of my grandmother, I never had the opportunity to learn. So I stood in knee-deep water by myself watching the rest of the children jumping and splashing in the waves. Little did I know that earlier that day, during low tide, some beachgoers had dug a hole close to the shoreline to make a sandcastle. Since then, the tide had come in and hidden this danger from me as I played in the shallows. The next thing I knew, I sank into the trench, and the sea swallowed my entire body. I thrashed and slapped at the water, but no matter which way I moved, I could not get my footing to lift my head above the surface. I was drowning, panicking, trying to breathe without finding air. My heart pounded through the agonizing seconds, but my mind went blank. I had no plan, no hope.

At that moment I felt a strong hand grip my upper arm and pull me back to higher ground. Coughing, choking, and crying, I realized a man had rescued me from certain death. Not having seen my near drowning and this man's timely rescue, my cousins came rushing over, suspicious of the stranger's intentions when they spotted him with me. I do not recall having ever said one word to him or vice versa, but my cousins took me to where my aunts were, and the man disappeared from my life.

Or *did* he?

After I told my aunts what had happened, they made me stay on the blanket for the rest of our time at the beach while my cousins continued to play in the surf. I wanted to join in on the fun, but I felt I was being punished for something that was not my fault.

While I didn't have friends outside of my family, I did have some special ones inside of that circle. From my mother's first marriage, I had a half brother, Sonny, and a half sister, Nanci. Nanci was seventeen years older than me, and every Saturday for as long as I could remember, she would come to the house to wash and style my grandmother's hair for the week. I loved seeing Nanci. She was always loving toward me and never forgot to bring me a toy or treat. When Mom would force her to cut my hair and bangs ridiculously short, Nanci would be near tears, telling me she was sorry.

The Sundays Mom and I spent with my mother, father, and Michael were also special. I can't say they brought me closer to my parents, but I loved being with my brother. We particularly enjoyed going across the street to Uncle Ralph's farm where an adventure always awaited us, sometimes as exciting as getting to ride his horses.

My cousin Madeline, who was just three months older than me, was my favorite. She was actually the first grandchild chosen to stay with Mom, but when she did not stop crying for three straight days, my aunts had decided to send her home and bring me in as her replacement. Madeline was an only child, and the Sunday afternoons when she came over with her parents were always the best. After dinner, Madeline and I would head over to the pharmacy to buy candy. After a few turns and half-blocks, we would hit the jackpot—Rock Candy®, Bag of Gold™ gum, Bit-O-Honey®, and Sugar Babies®. Sometimes, Madeline would sleep over, and we would hide our treats under our pillows so we could share sweets and stories through the night.

Seemingly not long after our candy-eating days, we were in high school together. It was a small private Catholic girl's school, but we traveled in different circles. Madeline's friends were from her neighborhood near the school. As a commuter, I made friends with the other girls on the train to school. Interacting with friends I made catapulted me into teenage rebellion. I gave Mom a difficult time about what I felt were excessive restrictions on my life. The tipping point came when I was turned down for the National Honor Society. I had worked so hard to earn the qualifying grades, but the necessary community service and leadership points were difficult to come by because Mom would not allow me to stay after school to participate in extracurricular activities or clubs. I had *had* it. The screaming match that had resulted from this drama ended with Mom dropping me off at my parents' house and me telling my parents, "I'm not going back, not ever!"

In the weeks that followed, some of my aunts and uncles tried bribing me to return to Mom's with all sorts of promises that I knew would never be kept. I dug in. Besides, I was finally living with my mother and father and, the best part of all, with my brother, Michael.

After graduating from high school, my first choice was to go away to college, but it was a barrier that women had not yet broken in my traditional family. I cannot remember many of my male cousins going away to school either. Mom's insistence on education, however, paid off for me because I was able to secure a spot in the highly selective nursing program at Fairfield University, a short commute from our house.

My college years were good and bad. Being a commuter was good because I could see my extended family on a regular basis, and despite vowing to never move back in with her, I still went to see Mom every week. I also met a fellow commuter and nursing student, Donna Diaz, who would become my dearest lifelong friend. We were inseparable.

On the sad end of the spectrum, my dad's commercial development company was forced into bankruptcy, which caused a major rift between my parents, ending in their ultimate separation. As a result, I was only able to see my dad about once a month. With the family's financial struggles mounting, my mother pressured me to work long hours as an aide at the hospital in addition to my demanding coursework as a nursing student. Yet none of that stopped me from loving Dad with all my heart.

My sophomore year at Fairfield University was not all gloom. In fact, it was one of the best years of my life because it was the year I met a handsome senior while working on a group project for my sociology class.

Gerry Michaud had brown hair and a brown mustache, twinkling hazel eyes, and a friendly disposition that energized the people around him. He was the captain of the hockey team, and I ended up being a cheerleader. We hit it off immediately and began dating soon after. Gerry graduated the end of that school year, but he stayed at Fairfield to pursue his master's in psychology as well as our relationship.

After two years of dating, we saw each other with increasing frequency, which meant spending time with my family. Gerry got everyone's approval, even Mom's, though she quipped she gave her blessing *despite* his not being Italian. During our visits, my aunts and uncles always opined that Mom had never been the same since I had left. That made me sad, and I understood their increased concerns for her well-being, especially after Mom was diagnosed with metastatic cancer, and all we could do was keep her comfortable.

Coincidentally, I had been assigned Dr. Elisabeth Kübler-Ross's groundbreaking book *On Death and Dying* for one of my classes in nursing school. Death was always a topic that made me fearful, and although the shadow of my grandmother's death loomed large, I skipped the reading. However, I found through the class lectures that Dr. Kübler-Ross's spiritual take on death and the afterlife fit with my Christian upbringing and gave me comfort. When my aunts called to tell me that Mom was lingering in a coma and they thought she was waiting for me before she died, I was prepared to visit.

When I walked into her bedroom, I harbored no ill feelings toward my grandmother for the rough times. I was sad and, more than that, I felt sorry for her. She had lost her husband over thirty years ago and had never adjusted. With the demands of raising twelve children, she had not found time for a social life and did not have many friends. Instead, she cried over my grandfather almost every day. Whenever she picked up the life-sized picture of him in her family room or after one of the many funerals she attended in our large Italian community, she would cry as if he had just died yesterday. As a child it seemed that growing up meant your spouse died and you spent the rest of your life crying over that loss. That Christ died and rose again on the third day was missing. Hope was missing.

As I sat in a chair next to the old four-poster bed that I had shared with Mom for twelve years, I held her hand and told her it was okay. Trusting she could hear me, I thanked her for doing her best in raising me. I told her I loved her and that we would all be fine. It was important to me to tell her that she was loved and that she could go. After an emotionally charged visit, I left with tears still glistening in my eyes. Two hours later, my hope that Mom had heard me seemed to be answered. I received the call that Mom, the woman who had raised me for twelve years, had died. Mom's death left another empty space in my heart.

After graduation, I planned to move with Gerry close to his home in New Hampshire. The Dartmouth/Hitchcock Medical Center accepted me into its Nurse Anesthesia program, but days before we were to move, the boys' prep school on the Fairfield University's campus offered Gerry a senior counseling position. So I moved near Gerry's hometown while he stayed in mine. Fortunately, Donna Diaz accepted a job at the medical center where I would be attending graduate school, so we roomed together and savored our good times.

After two years of long-distance love, I graduated, and a month later Gerry and I were married. Life grew ever more wonderful from that point on. Back at home I took a position at a local hospital where I was a nurse anesthetist and coordinated the continuing education and quality assurance programs for the Anesthesia Department. Gerry rose in the ranks at Fairfield Prep until he was dean of student services. Outside of work, we were inseparable.

Gerry had always been interested in the martial arts. When he signed up for Taekwondo classes, he met John Berger, a tall, broad-shouldered man with a stern brow that eased with his quick wit. It was not long before I was taking the classes too. Gerry and John grew close and spent countless hours together in and out of the dojo. They even discussed opening a business together, and their friendship led to occasional double dates between John, his wife, Jane, and Gerry and me.

After several years of marriage, Gerry and I had not had any children, which concerned my dad. When I would see him, he would always ask, "When are you gonna have children?"

Gerry and I were both young and enjoying life. We didn't feel in a rush, but I always said, "Dad, soon."

Within the year, I learned that my dad's wish had come true. I was pregnant. The heartbreak was that the news came two months after my father died of a massive heart attack at only fifty-seven years of age. The largest empty space in my heart yet. I was devastated, but in the midst of my anguish, I had a dream about my father that brought me some peace. He was in his suit and tie like always, but there was this ethereal glow about his entire body. He looked so happy; every line of worry was erased from his face and he was beaming. His entire visage was completely transformed, and that vision of my father gives me great solace even to this day.

Learning that I was pregnant only months after Dad's death and knowing how badly he had wanted grandchildren confused all my emotions. I had overwhelming joy at the prospect of bringing a new life into this world, but, at the same time, I was devastated and mourning the loss of my dad. Not only was I filled with grief but my father's death also made me acutely aware of my own mortality. My grandmother and my dad had passed, and my generation was next in succession. I began to develop an even deeper fear of death, especially when I gave birth to our daughter.

Dawn Marie Michaud was greeted by two exhilarated parents. I thought I understood true, all-encompassing love from the way I loved Gerry, but the feeling I had when I heard Dawn's cry and first laid eyes on my baby girl was beyond compare. She was the love of my life, so utterly filling my heart that I did not know if I would ever have enough space left over to fit another soul inside it. Our friends John and Jane experienced this bliss less than a year later when their child, Laura, was born. We were convinced that we were at the beginning of a journey of lifelong friendship, not just between the adults but also between our newborn daughters as well.

The days began tumbling over one another. Shortly after Laura was born, I learned I was pregnant again. Gerry and I were overjoyed. We began to prepare and looked forward to having another child. It was not until weeks before the due date that I grew concerned. It was late at night, and I was rocking Dawn in the peaceful hush of her nursery when I was suddenly overcome with emotion. There I sat with this beautiful child with whom I had shared a special bond for two years, and in less than a month, that bond would be changed forever. I would have another child to care for, and I feared that with how much I loved Dawn, there would be no room left in my heart for this newcomer. My newborn child would be stealing away some of my love and attention from Dawn.

When my baby brother had been born, I was sent away to live with my grandmother because two children would be a burden to my recovering mother. There was no way I would ever send my Dawnie away, but the impending birth of my second baby cast the shadow of my childhood abandonment over me and dredged up that sadness.

When Gerard Stephen Michaud, whom we called Stephen after my dad, was born, I laughed at how silly my concerns had been. Immediately I knew I would have no problem making room in my heart for Stephen and that I would love him just as much as I loved Dawn.

In time, we moved to a home that could accommodate our growing family in Trumbull, a wonderful community where we found our niche. The children were enrolled in school, and Gerry and I were active in the church and school system. Dawn's teacher said that Dawn was everyone's friend, and our phone was ringing off the hook with requests for playdates with Stephen. Gerry and I still juggled hectic work schedules, housekeeping, and personal and family commitments, but there was so much more to do. Dawn and Stephen were in Sunday school, the Christmas pageant, and the children's choir. They both started skating lessons, and we became "rink parents." We also made time for the country petting farm on Sunday, armed with breadcrumbs left over from the week, and walks to the duck pond or playground after school. We went strawberry picking in the summer, to the pumpkin patch and for hayrides in the fall, and tramping through the woods to cut down our own Christmas tree.

I had missed so many of these family opportunities when I was a child that I probably overcompensated with my children. Growing up with Mom, I never experienced the magical moments of childhood. There was no Santa Claus. When I was old enough to understand the concept of Santa, I would wake up early on Christmas morning and rush to the living room, but there were never any presents under the tree. I never had a birthday party either. Those missed experiences were so demoralizing for me as a child that I simply would not let that happen with my own children. Whether apple picking, trick-or-treating, or having a birthday party, I would not let the busyness of life interfere. Gerry and I were committed to each other and placed our family above all of life's urgent trivialities. I began to really take notice of how God was taking the negatives I had experienced in my past and was weaving them together to bless my life.

Amid all the hustle and bustle, our good friends John and Jane divorced in 1986. Gerry carved out time from his schedule to be there for John. Sometimes, John would come to the house just needing to talk and have someone around to listen, and Gerry spent a great deal of time supporting him through this difficult period. Not only had the divorce affected John emotionally but it also weighed on him at work where he was in charge of his family's mechanical contracting business. Gerry suggested he take some time off and consider changing course, so John took a break from the family business to take a job in law enforcement. John and Gerry grew incredibly close, and I knew if Gerry was "missing," all I had to do to find him was to give John a call.

Several years had passed when our son Michael was born. He may have been unplanned, but beauty in life often comes from the unexpected. His arrival did bring about a change in course for us. With an extra mouth to feed, Gerry decided to make a career change to better provide for our family. After months of planning, and with the help of my brother, Michael, we opened our first VideoTime store. With three small children and a new business venture, I cut back my hours at the hospital to a few days a week. VideoTime became a real family business. Gerry was successful in his first try at running a business and was able to open a small video production company and a second VideoTime store.

Life could not have been better, and we were truly thankful for all our blessings. Dawn had grown into a lovely young girl, with beautiful long hair and big, shining blue eyes. She loved the stories I would bring home from the operating room, and she decided that she wanted to be a hand surgeon like one of the doctors I frequently worked with. Of course, she also wanted to be an Olympic skater and spent many hours after school and on the weekends working toward her dream.

Then there was rough-and-tumble Stephen. He was such a character, and he loved to play hockey, just like his daddy. Kind-hearted Stephen looked the most like my side of the family, and he was very good with his hands, always building some architectural wonder out of his Lego® set.

Finally, there was little Michael. Mischief seemed to be his middle name, yet he was so intuitive, his teachers would marvel at how quickly a child his age could complete intricate puzzles.

It was such a joy to have three precious children in my life, but it was also a handful. My sister, Nanci, who loved the kids, was always willing to pitch in and babysit or cook a meal. "Uncle Mike" would take Dawn and Stephen fishing, bribing them with ice cream and cheeseburgers until they began to enjoy the actual activity just as much as he did.

Then there was John. Laura had gone to live with her mother in Chicago, but John got to see her eight weeks out of the year. Being a young, single male, John's daily life did not provide many fun opportunities for a little girl. So, over the summer, he would happily take Laura, Dawn, and Stephen to the beach, movies, or other family-friendly activities. Thanks to all those collective efforts, Gerry and I were able to spend some time alone. Or, if Gerry was busy with the stores, it would at least afford me the luxury of relaxing and playing the piano for an hour. I had taken years of lessons, and while I was not hugely proficient, nothing could bring me peace like playing classical music.

Gerry and I were believers, and we were grateful to God for everything in our lives. Practicing our faith in God was never a question; it was just what we did. We all knew Jesus and followed the customs of worship in our church. My knowledge of God was solid, but the routine of our religious practice could allow for complacency of the heart. When I began to sing in the adult choir on Sundays, I first heard a whisper of something more. I just didn't know what.

Despite my belief in God and His promise of eternal life, I had never been able to shake the real fear of death that began after Dawn's birth. The first truly frightening experience occurred when I was busy in the kitchen preparing dinner while waiting for the school bus. Suddenly, I got this sensation that traveled from the top of my head through every part of my body, all the way to my fingertips and toes. The feeling was unmistakable. The blood in my veins had turned to ice, and the singular thought that coursed through my mind was *What would you do if all your children were dead?* For what felt like the longest moment, I was paralyzed and unable to breathe. It was as if I was five years old and back in the ocean drowning. When I finally managed to take a gulp of air and calm down, I instantly began rationalizing. *How ridiculous*, I thought.

I forced a long, slow exhale as if breathing out the terrifying intrusive thoughts. I momentarily shuddered and forced the thought from my consciousness. Then the school bus pulled up.

Twice more I was assailed by this harbinger of death. Each time, I was lying in bed, just about to drift off to sleep, when my heart began to pound, and death again crept into my heart and my thoughts. As soon as it hit me, I sat bolt upright, gasping for air. While I had fears over my children's deaths during that first gut-wrenching episode, I now thought it was my own death that was imminent. I thought maybe I was sick. Maybe I had cancer. The fear grew so overwhelming that I decided to seek counseling. I simply could not continue living like this.

Despite my increasing anxiety, we were wrapping up a terrific summer. We were just about to move into our dream home, and we had planned a family trip to Florida. The counseling would have to wait. Maybe a little vacation was all I needed.

HEART OF
THE MATTER

We all don't get to fight lions and bears, but like David, the Lord always prepares us for what He calls us to in life. God doesn't leave anything to chance. He uses our hurts, disappointments, and missteps to build up the strength and resilience we need to get through the coming night. He gets us where we need to be. He tells us what to do once we get there, and all He asks is for us to listen and trust.

Finally, be strong in the Lord and in the strength of his might.

—Ephesians 6:10 ESV

CHAPTER 2

Facing the Unimaginable

A time to weep, And a time to laugh;
A time to mourn, And a time to dance.

—Ecclesiastes 3:4 NKJV

It was a sunny day on the Connecticut Turnpike as John Berger drove his daughter, Laura, and her two friends, Dawn and Stephen Michaud, to the skating rink. Summer was ending, and this would be one of the last days John spent with his daughter and her friends before Laura returned to her mother's house in Chicago and the Michauds left for Florida. Trips to the skating rink had been a highlight of the summer. This day was no exception.

"Uncle John," Dawn called from the back seat, where all three children sat, "Laura doesn't have her seat belt on."

John's eyes glinted at Laura's reflection in his rearview mirror. "Laura, put on your seat belt."

"I can't, it's stuck in the seat," Laura said.

"All right," John replied, "I'll pull over to the side of the road and help you get it out."

"No, Uncle John, don't do that," Dawn said in a monotone voice unlike her own. "A truck could hit us and push the gas tank into the back seat, and it would explode. We would all burn to death."

Shocked by the eight-year-old's response, John said nothing but heeded the warning and kept driving.

Dawn's uncharacteristic words disturbed John the rest of the day. When he saw Gerry later that afternoon, John told him the story and said, "Gerry, that was some strange stuff Dawn was saying and I just have a bad feeling about this trip to Florida. It's like an omen or a warning. I don't think you should go."

Gerry chuckled. "Who knows what they're teaching kids in school these days," he said. "Don't worry, everything's going to be fine."

August started out as a hectic month. We were working through some details with the sellers of our new house, packing up our old house, finishing renovations on our store, and keeping up with the kids' busy schedules. Dawn was skating three or four times a week at crazy hours. Stephen, the social butterfly, was always being invited out or inviting in. Michael, my little sweetheart, thankfully was content being my shadow and playing with his Batman and Ninja Turtle "guys." Everyone needed a vacation, and our trip on August 12, Gerry's birthday, could not arrive soon enough.

Our vacation would be perfect. The children would spend all day in a circus workshop, swinging on the flying trapeze and being entertained with magic tricks and clowns, while Gerry and I would relax by the pool or on the beach. When the circus workshop wrapped up for the day, we would have quality family time without the distractions of daily life at home.

We began moving into our home in Trumbull three days prior to our trip to Florida. The first two days were filled with unpacking and settling in, and the children could not stop showing off their new rooms to anyone who came by. Michael was so proud to have a room of his own even though at night he was tucking back in with his big brother Stephen to sleep. We would all take a while to adjust to the change, but Gerry and I were thrilled to finally have made the move.

On the evening of August 11, my sister, Nanci, and her fiancé, Augie, came over to help with last-minute preparations. Nanci brought goodie bags for the children, which only added to their already monumental excitement. Then she helped me with some last-minute details. We bathed the children, brushed their hair and teeth, and got them to bed. Nanci always loved brushing Dawn's long, beautiful hair. When the children were in bed, the house bustled with the adults' excitement over the upcoming trip. Augie and Gerry set up our new bed while Nanci and I finished packing.

That night, as Gerry and I lay in bed talking, we spoke of how our hard work had paid off in providing for our family. We had to budget our resources, but we were rich in our love for each other and in having three healthy children, food on our table, and a roof over our heads. For that, we felt truly blessed and thankful, and savoring our happiness, we made love one last time before we drifted off to sleep.

The alarm sounded at 5 a.m., and Gerry said, "Donna, you better get going, the car will be here soon."

When I walked into their rooms, Dawn and Stephen were already up and dressed, abuzz with excitement over their upcoming adventure. My Dawnie, glowing in her pink-and-blue outfit, asked if I would braid her hair, and Stephen, being all boy, asked when we would eat. As I braided Dawn's hair, I told Stephen that we would have breakfast on the plane. I waited until the last moment to scoop Michael out of bed and get him dressed. Through his sleepiness, he prattled away about his first time on an airplane.

The flight from New York was uneventful, but things did not go as planned when we reached Palm Beach International Airport. After retrieving our bags and catching the shuttle, we learned the original car we had reserved was unavailable, so we had to wait for a replacement. The children and I gazed out at the sunny Florida landscape through the ceiling to floor plate-glass windows lining the car rental office, until, at last, Gerry returned with the contracts, maps, and keys.

"This is farther than the travel agent told us, but don't worry, I've got maps and directions," he said.

We got into the car, a brown, four-door, Mercury Marquis and exited the airport toward I-95. In Connecticut, I-95 is called "the Turnpike," so we followed the signs, drove down Okeechobee Boulevard, and entered the Turnpike North. Not long after, we realized that I-95 in Florida was not the Turnpike, so Gerry pulled to a stop on the side of the highway several miles past the PGA Boulevard exit to check his map and directions.

August 12 was a bright, sunny day in Fairfield, Connecticut, and Michael Schinella, a tan, fit, thirty-three-year-old commercial developer was home enjoying Chinese takeout with his wife, Jody, and their one-year-old son, Michael Jr. They had just finished their meal when the doorbell rang. Michael answered the door to find a young, uniformed police officer looking shaken.

"Is this the Schinella residence?" the police officer asked.

"Yes, sir," Michael replied.

"Are you Michael Schinella?"

"What's going on?"

"We've received a call from the Jupiter Police Department in Florida. There's been an accident."

"What happened?"

The young officer could not say, and cold sweat formed on Michael's back as the policeman kept repeating what little information he had. My brother could not help but feel panic, and after numerous attempts at questioning the officer, Michael was able to ascertain that the accident involved me, but each time he asked about me, Gerry, or the kids' well-being, the young policeman failed to conjure up the nerve to answer. Michael's anxiety and confusion grew. *They had to be okay*, he thought. *They just moved into their new house and they still had boxes to unpack. Gerry just sold one video store and opened another. They all celebrated my birthday just a few nights before, and they had been so happy and excited about their long-awaited vacation.*

Finally, the young officer's supervisor, Sergeant Ed Riley, arrived to deliver the news. He confirmed that I had indeed been in an accident and was the lone survivor.

Devastation struck. In shock, Michael scrambled to call our older half brother, Sonny, to relay the news and discuss ways to get to Florida while still trying to gather as much information as possible from the policemen. Little did he know, all he had to do was turn on the television, and he would have seen the helicopters circling the wreckage and reporters delivering updates. In panic mode, Jody took Michael Jr. to her bedroom and prayed. Then she packed a bag for him, and her mother picked him up. After speaking to Sonny, Michael called our sister, Nanci, and before long, everyone had gathered at Michael's house.

Nanci was beside herself. She kept running along the side and back of the house repeating the same cry, "I was just with them. I was just with them." She had just given little Dawn a shower the night before. She thought of how Dawn had tilted her head back to let the water run through her long hair and how she had looked up at Nanci with her big, blue eyes and asked, "Aren't I beautiful, Aunt Nanci?"

Jody called the nurses at Jupiter Hospital and learned that I was being airlifted to Shands Hospital in Gainesville where they had the best facility in the area to care for my extensive burns. With no direct air route to Gainesville and having no luck with commercial flights, the family did not want to lose six or more hours to reach me. So Sonny reached out to a friend at a nearby private airport, and, understanding the urgency, his friend immediately offered to provide the family with a chartered flight to reach me. In the throes of shock and grief, Michael, Jody, Nanci, and Augie prepared to leave, having no idea whether I'd still be alive by the time they got there.

The flight was surreal, and the group of mourners did not get to the hotel adjoined to Shands Hospital in Gainesville until 12:30 a.m. Michael thought they would not be able to get into the burn unit until morning, but Nanci insisted they try. So they tossed their bags in their rooms, walked across the hotel lobby and through the covered connector to the hospital, went up the elevator, and down the hallway to the burn intensive care unit, where they were greeted by a team of nurses. Before they could enter, the nurses assisted them in dressing head to toe in sterile gowns, masks, caps, and booties, and apprised them of the situation.

"Burn patients like Donna have to deal with the most severe pain," one of the nurses said. "We've been giving her intravenous morphine and Versed to help her relax, but there's something you should know: Whether it's the Versed or the enormity of the trauma, Donna is suffering from retrograde amnesia. She doesn't remember anything about the accident. When she sees you, she is going to ask about her family. One of you needs to be prepared to answer her."

Nanci was too distraught to take on such a task, so Michael accepted the responsibility.

The nurse led Michael, Jody, Nanci, and Augie into the burn ICU. The smell was enough to make them gag, and the walls were splattered with blood and the different ointments and solutions used to clean and treat burns. They passed several doors in the hallway before the nurse showed them into my room, and they could not believe what they saw. Lying motionless on the bed, I was wrapped in bandages from head to toe. My arms were suspended in the air as if I were playing an invisible, floating piano. Plugged into machines by myriad tubes, my body was so swollen from fluid retention from the trauma, common with burns, that my head was the size of a basketball.

"That's our sister?" Nanci asked.

Michael walked to my side and said as calmly as he could, "Donna, it's Michael. Lift your finger if you can understand me."

"Donna, it's Nanci. I'm here. You're going to be okay."

Heavily sedated, I did not respond.

The nurse suggested that I might be more alert in the morning, so the four of them returned to the hotel, got a few hours of restless sleep, and returned early the next morning. They adhered to the same scrubbing routine as the night before and followed the nurse to my room. I was awake this time and reached toward them. Michael and Nanci came to my side to console me.

"We're here for you," Michael said. "You're going to be okay. You're going to be fine."

I could not speak with the endotracheal tube down my throat but motioned with my arm. As best I could with all the bandages, I extended my hand out and then lowered it twice as if descending two steps. At first, no one understood, so I repeated the motion, sticking my hand out at three different, distinct heights. Suddenly, everyone knew who I was asking about. Nanci burst into tears, and Michael ushered everyone out the door. Augie took Nanci down the hall, and Jody stayed nearby to offer support, should Michael need it. He turned back into the room and walked to my bed. With the bandages on my face, Michael could hardly see anything more than my eyes, and he could not even hold my hand or hug me before the breaking the gut-wrenching news.

Again, I motioned for the three children.

Michael held his breath as the tears formed in his eyes. It was the hardest thing he ever had to do in his life. "Donna—" He choked on the lump in his throat. "Gerry and the children—" Michael paused, trying to summon the strength to continue, "didn't survive the accident."

I went limp as I sobbed, and tears streamed down the bandages on my face. Michael could see that my entire world had just crumbled. Neither he nor Nanci, Jody, or Augie could imagine the feelings trapped inside my broken heart and battered body, and they were helpless to do anything about it. They could only spend the day watching the tears soak the bandages on my face.

John Berger had worked the night shift and had been asleep for less than an hour when pounding on his back door startled him awake. He hopped out of bed, grabbed the sidearm he carried every day as a police officer, and headed downstairs for the door. Lenny, a fireman friend of his, was holding up his newspaper and yelling.

Looking at the newspaper, John asked, "What? What happened?"

Lenny shouted. "Gerry's dead!"

"What? Gerry's dead? Get outta here, I just saw Gerry two days ago!"

"He's dead, look!" Lenny shouted, shoving the newspaper into John's chest as he pushed his way into the house.

THE ACCIDENT SITE

Photo courtesy of the Palm Beach Sheriff's Office, West Palm Beach, FL

In the aftermath of the collision and the inferno it caused, it was difficult to tell the blackened car from the asphalt.

The two men sat at the kitchen table, and John read the article. It said that a tractor-trailer had run over our vehicle, flipped onto its side, and skidded to a stop. Our car had burst into flames twenty feet high, and eyewitnesses said that as I began to crawl through the shattered windshield, two men urged me forward. They pulled me away from the car, but I fought to run back to it, screaming, "My family! My family! My whole life is in that car!" While the driver and passenger in the tractor-trailer had survived, my husband and three children had not.

When he finished the article, John dropped the newspaper on the table. "I don't believe this," he said. "Listen. I've got to fly down there. Right now."

Lenny agreed and left as John began calling the airlines. After his divorce, John had canceled his credit cards, and the airlines were not letting him buy a ticket without one, which turned into an hour-and-a-half ordeal that was driving John crazy. In the midst of the chaos, he received a call from my cousin Madeline.

"Did you hear?" Madeline asked. "I have to get down there!"

"Yeah, I'm trying to get a ticket," John said.

"Don't worry about that, I'll get the tickets. I just got off the phone with Michael. He said they're at Shands Hospital in Gainesville."

"Shands Hospital? What about the crash site? These guys could make mistakes. I gotta get down there. They could've screwed this up. Gerry could be alive! You don't know what they've done."

"No," Madeline replied, "Michael wants us to go to Shands. It's been so long since I spoke with Donna, but I just have to see her." Shortly after, John and Madeline met at the airport and made the arduous trip to Gainesville to visit me in the hospital.

Madeline's and my relationship remained close until our early thirties when Madeline's difficult divorce drove a wedge between us. She expressed her concern to John that I might not want to see her. John, on the other hand, had never been close to me. He only knew me as Gerry's wife and a former karate student. If anything, John would give Gerry a good-natured ribbing for the times I called his house looking for my husband. Aside from the occasional double dates before John's divorce and the times after his divorce when John took the kids or would stop by on a holiday, we hardly conversed, and we didn't know each other well. While John empathized greatly with me, all he could think about was his friend Gerry and getting to the crash site to see for himself what had happened. Instead, he went with Madeline to Shands Hospital. On their way, they decided that John would visit me first and Madeline would wait for his update before seeing me.

Being a police officer, John had been on calls at the burn unit of his city hospital. He had experienced the smell and had seen the walls stained with silver nitrate splatters. What could be a startling scene of frantic people crying over their badly injured loved ones was not unfamiliar to John.

When he entered my room fully gowned with a mask, hat, gloves, and shoe covers, the scene did not shock him, but it was as horrific as he had anticipated, maybe more so. John had always been the type of guy who had something to say in any situation—a comment to get people who had fallen into complacency on their toes or a joke to lighten the mood—but what he saw and felt left him speechless. Michael, Jody, and

Augie were standing in stunned silence, while Nanci patted away her tears. Undoubtedly, they were all in shock that someone they loved could look the way I did. John stood watching for a moment with no clue as to why he was there or what he should be doing to help. Then he looked at my face, and at that point he heard a voice, not his own voice, but a voice in his head that clearly said, "Take care of this woman."

As a child, instead of being spoiled as the youngest, John had been neglected, and he often prayed for God to help him. When he was about six years old, John told his mother that Jesus had promised him that if he followed and served Him that Jesus would always take care of him. John could still remember his mother saying, "I believe you, son, but don't ever tell anybody about that."

Standing at the foot of the bed that day, John looked around for the source of the voice, but he knew in his heart that it belonged to God. As he looked at me, he thought there was no way I could survive. My head was the size of a basketball; my face was unrecognizable. My fingernails were all burned off, and surgical staples were holding my fingers together. I was swathed in bandages, and the smell in the room was jarring. It was the smell of people who would die or be scarred for life. He shook his head and thought to himself, *No, I don't want to do that. I don't want to take on that burden. That's not right. I don't think I should have to do that.*

John had been divorced for four years and had adjusted to being by himself. There were obvious drawbacks to being alone, but he had grown to like his life. He was free to come and go as he pleased without ever having to check in with or answer to anyone. Being single, he had the freedom to pack up and leave whenever he liked, and he had plans to settle in California where he would spend the rest of his life enjoying the beach and the beautiful weather. Taking care of me was definitely not a part of those plans.

Then John heard the voice again: "Take *care* of this woman."

But that time he did not just hear the voice. Practicing martial arts, John knew what a solid punch felt like, but this was a punch in the stomach like he had never felt, and it knocked the wind out of him. He looked at me again and almost dropped to his knees. He could not catch his breath and thought to himself, *I've got to get out of here.*

With that, John turned back to the door, walked outside, leaned over with his hands on his knees, and took a couple of deep breaths.

A nurse quickly approached and asked, "Are you all right?"

"Yes, I just need a glass of orange juice," he said, still doubled over and taking deep breaths.

"It's okay. This happens all the time," she said as she put his arm around her shoulder.

Perhaps, but not to John Berger. As the nurse led John to a nearby chair, she had no idea of the struggle that was ensuing in his mind and soul. His head was spinning as he thought, *If I take care of her, I will have to devote my life to her. There would be no freedom to move to California. Forget about a girlfriend or wife.*

This was a huge sacrifice, a monumental, life-altering decision that he never, ever considered he would encounter when he boarded that plane to Florida. But the spiritual power in that voice led him to his decision.

After sitting for a few minutes and downing the orange juice that the nurse had brought, he answered the voice in his head, "All right, I'll do it. I'll do my best to take care of her."

John was resolute in his decision when he returned to my room. It certainly did not look like I would make it, and if I did, I was sure to have severe lifelong disabilities. But whatever the outcome, his mind was at ease in obeying God's call. He walked to my side and stooped down to whisper in my ear.

"Listen," he told me, "if you live . . . I will take care of you."

As he walked back to the end of the bed, a sense of calm came over him, and he felt like himself again. He reevaluated the scene, and as he took it in, his eyes landed on the sheet covering my feet. Feeling curious and comfortable in his own skin again, he lifted the sheet and quipped, "Your toes look good!"

HEART OF THE MATTER

Before we are even aware of what has befallen us, there is in us an unconscious awareness of the presence of God. He is before us, and He is behind us. He is there in our darkness, and when we awake, He is still there with us. Before we are even able to think of forming a syllable of prayer, God knows and hears us cry out to Him.

Even before a word is on my tongue,
behold, O LORD, you know it altogether.

—PSALM 139:4 ESV

Friends, it is usually only in the rearview mirror that we can see the faithful presence of the Lord during a time of disaster.

But be assured He is all-knowing and ever-present, unfolding His plan for our survival and recovery even in the midst of the unthinkable.

CHAPTER 3

Where Am I?

My eyes are blinded by my tears. Each day I beg for your help,
O LORD; I lift my hands to you for mercy.

—Psalm 88:9 NLT

My heart was racing so fast it jerked me up off my pillow as I gasped for air in my sea of uncontrollable panic. Fear flowed through my veins, warning me that something horrific was about to happen—but it already had. My consciousness was out of sync as it dashed between parallel universes, caught in the past yet knowing the tragic future. Gerry and the kids were dead. I can't remember how I found out, but I woke up and I knew. My brain struggled to make sense of it all through the fog of catastrophe and sedation.

Then the pain shocked me into clarity: indescribable physical pain and emotional anguish. It had been three, maybe four days before I could commit to memory the fragments of my life and slowly piece together my reality. Something had happened on our way to Club Med on Sandpiper Bay in Florida. I remembered getting the rental car, and then only snapshots—Gerry slumped over the steering wheel in his short-sleeved plaid shirt with his face turned toward me, his expression peaceful, as if he were asleep. Unrelenting heat scorching my face and hair, bringing my hands up in front of my face as if they could stop the burning. Hearing our son Michael in the back seat,

37

shrieking. A feeling of exhaustion from my own screams that sounded like a distant echo.

Then, everything went black.

It was my husband's thirty-seventh birthday, and he and our three precious children died that day in a rental car on the shoulder of the Florida Turnpike.

I saw my brother, Michael, standing next to a man in a white coat at the foot of my hospital bed, and I tried to speak, but the tube down my throat swallowed my words. My focus drifted down to see white gauze dressings covering the third-degree burns on my arms and hands. Both of my hands were fanned in plaster splints that extended beyond my fingers. A pencil was taped to the splint on my left hand so I could spell out words by pointing to letters on an alphabet board that a nurse held up for me.

"W" . . . "H" . . .

"Who?" the occupational therapist asked.

I shook my head no.

"What?" he asked.

Again, I shook my head no in frustration, wishing I could speak or at least spell out the whole word before being interrupted.

I began again. "W" . . . "H" . . . "E" . . . "R" . . . "E."

"Where," the occupational therapist said.

"G" . . . "E" . . . "R" . . . "R" . . . "Y."

"Gerry."

"K" . . . "I" . . .

"Where are Gerry and the kids?" the occupational therapist finally asked.

I nodded and turned to Michael. He swallowed hard and shook his head. It all came rushing back to me. If I had not been in a bed with my wrists strapped to the side rails to keep me from moving and tearing the tendons in my hands, I would have collapsed to the floor. I began to sob as the panic consumed me, but the endotracheal tube stole my sobs just as it stole my words. I was under water, drowning in my own silence with no foothold and no hope for air. My family was dead. In a mere nanosecond, in a single beat of my heart, my life had gone up in flames, leaving me collapsed amid a heap of smoldering ashes.

Through my silenced sobs, the discomfort of the endotracheal tube grew unbearable. I banged my foot on the side rail to get the attention of a nurse. One rushed in to check on me.

After a moment, he said, "You're breathing fine. Just try to relax."

The man standing next to Michael spoke. "Do you remember me, Donna?"

I shook my head.

"My name is Mike, like your brother. I'm a psychologist that works for the hospital. How much do you remember?"

Again, I shook my head. I couldn't remember anything. My training as a nurse made me aware that the events during an accident can happen too quickly for the brain to capture them, but I should have had *some* recall.

"That's okay, it's pretty normal with the drugs they've been giving you," Mike said. "It may come back in time. I'll try to fill you in as best I can. You're in the burn intensive care unit at Shands Hospital in Gainesville, Florida. You suffered multiple second- and third-degree burns, and the smoke inhalation caused you to develop pneumonia in both of your lungs. That tube down your throat is helping you breathe. You've had skin taken from your abdomen and upper thighs to graft onto your arms and hands. You're making good progress in your recovery, but it's going to take time. It's important for you to know that you are not alone in this. You have lots of people who love and care about you, and you've already received hundreds of letters from well-wishers praying for you to heal."

I could not comprehend it all. If I was there when Gerry and the kids had died, then I had to recall what happened. How could I not remember? It seemed impossible; they had to be okay. I kept picturing the moment when they would walk through that hospital room door and reveal all this as preposterous. If not for my excruciating physical pain, I could have believed my attempt at rationalization, but the agony of my injuries told me otherwise.

Later that day, the doctors felt my breathing had improved enough to take out the tube. What a relief. It was one thing to be intubated and sedated, quite another to be awake, desperately needing to communicate with those around you to connect the dots of memory and being unable to do so.

Being extubated also meant I graduated from having my burn injuries soaked and dressed in the hospital bed to traveling to the "tank room." The nurses wheeled my bed there and they submerged my entire body in the saltwater-filled "Hubbard tank." Pain stabbed my skin like thousands of tiny, poisoned needles pricking me all at once. After I soaked for a while, the nurses removed the bandages around my arms, shoulder, knee, and face as I moaned in pain. After the bandages were removed and the needle pricks had rendered my skin numb, the nurses drained the salt bath and cared for my grafted sites. They also debrided the non-grafted sites, cutting away the dead flesh and causing waves of nausea to swell within me. Once they were finished, they wrapped me in bandages again. I had been given pain medicine and sedatives before the tanking, but the combination was no match for this hellish experience.

It was in the tank room that I caught a fleeting glimpse of my face in a mirror for the first time since the accident. I was horrified. My head was swollen like a watermelon, and half of my nose was missing. Second-degree burns covered my face, and what was left of my hair was charred and matted. The severe burns Mike had described covered over 25 percent of my body. The third-degree burns were all grafted with skin from other areas of my body, while the second-degree burns were treated with special ointments. The deeper second-degree burns on my eyelids, nose, and right cheek were covered with porcine grafts, which were strips of skin taken from a baby pig that had been soaked in an antibacterial solution to ensure they were sterile. They were used to help prevent infection and scarring on the more severe burns on my face. When there was sufficient healing, the graft would just slough off on its own, much like any scab that had formed over an injury. One member of the staff tried to inject some humor by reassuring me that the only side effect of porcine grafts was a tendency to "oink," but I could only stare. The person I saw in the mirror could not be me. I was a healthy, attractive 35-year-old woman, not the grim funhouse-mirror image that I saw staring back at me.

Before long, I was fully wrapped again and left to wonder if I would ever look normal again. After that first tanking, I was rolled back to my room where my brother Michael and Mike, the psychologist, waited.

"Feeling better?" my brother asked.

I groaned in response. Mike, the psychologist, approached.

"Donna," Mike said, "there's something important we need to discuss. It is going to be difficult for you, but I promise we'll try to make it as painless as possible. Okay?"

I nodded, beginning to fade from the exhaustion of all the pain and medication.

"Okay," Mike said.

He turned to my brother, and Michael approached. "Hey, Donna," Michael said, holding his breath with an anxious look on his face. "We need to discuss the funeral. You're going to get through this and get well, but your injuries are severe, and it is hard to predict how long you will be here in the hospital. With winter on the horizon back home, we think it's best if we go forward with the funeral and burial before the ground freezes, but only if you agree to it."

As if I had been punched in the nose, my nostrils stung, and tears instantly streamed down my face.

"I know, I'm sorry," Michael said. "You don't need to worry about it. We're getting it all set, and John's helping us out. It will be at your church, and Gerry's friend Father Kelley is going to say the Mass. We've arranged to have it filmed so you'll have a tape of it. You have some important surgeries ahead of you to take care of all your injuries, and you need to put all your energy into getting better."

It was all too much. I just could not understand. What funeral? Gerry and the kids could not be gone.

"All we want to know," Michael said, "and then we don't have to talk about it anymore if you don't want to, is if there's anything special you want for the service or burial."

I tried to think about it, but thinking gave me a headache. What could I possibly do to show my husband and children how sad I was, how much I loved them? All I could think of was Gerry's time at Fairfield Prep and the beautiful voices of the men's chorus, so I somehow found the energy to say in a raspy, barely audible whisper, "Prep Singers."

"The Prep Singers?" Michael asked.

I nodded.

"The Fairfield Prep Singers," Michael repeated. "Absolutely, we can do that. Would you like to pick out the music?"

I nodded but felt so exhausted that I doubted I would have the energy or strength for such a task. But we went through the options, and somehow I chose our favorites, "Be Not Afraid," "Softly and Tenderly," "Here I Am, Lord," and "Nearer My God to Thee." Not long after ironing out those details, Michael flew home to attend to the funeral, but my best friend Donna Diaz flew down to stay with me. She offered me more than any words could: she offered the warm presence of a loving and faithful friend, and that was something I needed more than anything. It would be a while before I fully realized it, but the Lord in His faithfulness was already calling up an angel army to guide and protect me.

That first day of recalled consciousness passed by in agony. When I was not crying out from the physical pain, I would remember my strong husband and our three sweet children, and I mourned the loss of their lives with all of my heart, soul, and strength. We had so many more memories to make together. There should be birthdays, anniversaries, graduations, and weddings. Dawn might pursue her dream of being a doctor, and Stephen and Michael might follow in their dad's footsteps. They would all have families of their own, and we would have beautiful grandchildren. Gerry and I would grow old together, and we would retire. Sitting in our living room, we would reflect on our wonderful lives, and our hearts would overflow with the joy that God's blessings had provided us.

But that was all gone. Gerry and I would never grow old together. I would never plan another one of my children's birthdays; I would never see them grow an inch taller. I would never see Michael lose his first tooth, Stephen score his first goal, or Dawn skate in another competition. They were gone, and all the tears in the world could not bring them back, though that did not stop me from crying.

HEART OF
THE MATTER

Tears speak when we cannot. They say, "I feel so alone. I am overwhelmed with sorrow. I am collapsing under the weight of the pain I am suffering from my loss. A part of me has died." Tears are how our bodies respond to grief. Tears help us heal. In your grief, do what comes naturally: cry.

The tears streamed down and I let them flow
as freely as they would, making of them a pillow for my heart.
On them it rested.

—AUGUSTINE, *CONFESSIONS IX*, 12

Sleep eluded me that night. My wonderful night nurse, Linda, stayed up talking with me. I poured out all the pain in my heart, and she listened and tried to provide comfort, although there was no real comfort for what had happened. Around 3 a.m., she was called away to another room, and I was left alone. With no one left to cry out to, I turned to the cornerstone of my upbringing—my belief in God.

"Dear God, I don't know how this happened," I prayed. "I am so lost and alone and afraid. My heart feels like it has been torn in two. Why did you allow my family to die and leave me behind? Couldn't I have just had one to hold on to? I know it is not my will but Yours that I pray for, but I don't believe this was Your will. I know You can hear me. I am in so much pain that I think I am dying, too. Please help me."

Then, for the first time, I prayed a prayer that I would repeat endlessly.

"Lord, please take care of Gerry, Dawn, Stephen, and Michael, and tell them how much I love and miss them. And please help me because I'm not doing very well right now, and I need You to carry me because I'm not sure I can take another step."

After praying, I was still wide awake. For over eight years, I had not gone to sleep without tucking my children into bed and kissing my husband goodnight. I longed for their touch more than I had ever wanted anything in my life, but it was impossible. So I spoke to them.

"Gerry, how could this have happened? How could we be separated like this? Please take care of the children for me. I miss you so much! I love you. I've loved you from the moment I met you, and I'll never stop loving you. I'm so sorry this happened. I wish I could do something, *anything*."

More tears choked me, and I gave them time to run their course. Already I had learned that these tears would not be denied.

"Dawnie, my beautiful girl. I miss you so much! I was so happy to be your mommy. I'm sorry it was for such a short time, but I will always love you with all my heart.

"Stephen, my little buddy. You were such a good boy, so much like your daddy. I miss you to the moon and back. I love you so much, and I am so sorry for what has happened.

"Michael, my little Michael. How will I go on without you always by my side? I miss you and love you more than words can say."

I lay in my bed under a downpour of tears for a long while. I never knew that a broken heart could be so physically painful. My grief stood before me like a mountain blocking my path, and each tear fell like a tiny hammer on a sculptor's chisel and chipped away a single pebble of that mountain. But I had an ocean of tears and myriad piles of pebbles to go. And yet, in the throes of my pain, I was embraced by a feeling of gentle warmth. Was the Lord this soothing presence in my life?

When I finally fell asleep, I dreamed of Gerry. He was wearing the plaid shirt he had on the day of the accident, and he seemed to be at such great peace.

"Don't worry, Donna," he said. "You'll be with us in no time."

With that picture of Gerry in my mind and the sound of his calm voice in my head, I slept through what was left of that night.

I awoke the next morning and reflected on my beautiful dream. But when I thought about it, I was struck with a bout of paranoia. To be with them in no time, I would have to die soon.

I was in bad shape, and every second was a struggle to survive through all the pain. Could I die of an infection from my burns? I had received seven units of blood; could that have given me hepatitis or AIDS? My normally positive psyche couldn't stop perceiving everything as a potential disaster.

Although I felt my dream was telling me that I would die soon, oddly enough, I did not feel the same fear of death as I had before we left for our trip. In retrospect, I figured that my fear had been for my family's lives, not my own. When confronted with the aftermath of my closest brush with mortality, I did not have any episodes of ice in my veins, shortness of breath, or overwhelming thoughts of death. But, then again, could an outpouring of grace in those moments I spent near death have shown me that death was nothing to fear? The "Rock" on which I stood was sovereign and, in His hands, my spiritual and physical healing was already underway.

Later that day, Donna Diaz read through some of the mail I had received. It came from all over the country, and the mailman joked about just delivering the entire day's mail to my room and I could send back what wasn't mine. Many people shared their stories of losing children and how God pulled them through. They told me that I was not alone, that the Holy Spirit was filling me, and that God would scoop me up and carry me through. In addition to the letters, well-wishers sent mugs, plaques, drawings, and other items of encouragement, and I needed and deeply appreciated every thoughtful gesture.

As the days passed, I found myself struggling more and more with my physical injuries, and that difficulty gave me breaks from my grief. As strange as it sounds, it was as if God was using my catastrophic injuries to help pace me through my sorrow. When I could not feed myself or when a nurse was helping me use a bedpan because I could not walk to the bathroom, it was difficult to focus on my anguish.

Much of the time I was simply struggling to survive.

I was dealing with pneumonia in both lungs and the risk of life-threatening infection from my burns. On top of that, I had to undergo several surgeries on my hands if I were to have a prayer of ever being able to use them again. I needed additional grafting on my right knee and shoulder where the burns were too deep to heal on their own. Then there was the pain. In addition to the stinging and stabbing from my twice-daily saltwater tanking, debridement, and staple removal, there were electric-like jolts radiating up and down my arms as my nerves regenerated. I had aching muscles and the constant threat of bedsores from inactivity. The worst part of it was, there was no break, no rest from the constant assault. I could not even escape it through sleep, because my insomnia only allowed me to sleep about every other night, so even that offered only rare, fleeting moments of escape. The physical pain was impossible to ignore. It sidetracked my grief, leaving an ever-present storm cloud lurking in the recesses of my mind. Meanwhile, the morphine pump teased me with ever-so-fleeting moments of peace and relief that only distorted my reality.

Beyond the physical pain distracting me from my grief, I felt I had to be strong for my family and the people around me. Michael took the losses very hard, and Nanci could not go a minute without bursting into tears. The only thing that seemed to comfort them was to see me progressing. They were encouraged when I did well with my therapy, and they were battered with fresh waves of sadness whenever we tried to talk about the accident and I would break down. They filled me in as gently as they could with the details as they learned them, and the understanding I gleaned from those details was as vital toward my healing as the saltwater tanking and debridement.

Unfortunately, it was equally as painful.

My need to be strong only grew when Michael and Jody brought my mother to visit me after the funeral. She was in the beginning stages of Alzheimer's disease, and she was confused and emotional. My mother would talk about my deceased husband and children as if they were alive and could walk in at any moment, and then she would be sobbing over their losses when her memory returned. I didn't know how to console her.

With so much swirling around in my head, the last thing I needed to deal with was a change in my primary care nurse. Holly's replacement was named Charlie, and, at first, I was hesitant about having a male nurse. Charlie would be responsible for caring for me in some intimate ways, and I thought I would feel awkward and self-conscious about it. But Charlie was professional in every way, and his sharp sense of humor immediately put me at ease. We would have a cup of coffee and talk every morning before he would care for me, and as I got to know him and see more of him, his stature and mannerisms reminded me so much of Gerry. There was comfort and healing in being able to interact with Charlie. He was part of that angel army showing me that I would be able to move forward someday.

Throughout the thirty days I spent at Shands Hospital, I had many visitors. My sister Nanci and her daughter tended to my every need, constantly making trips to get things for me, feeding me, and reading me my mail. Donna Diaz was there for much of the time, too, and then there were all the doctors, nurses, therapists, and clergy, most of whom I interacted with daily. I believe they were all God-sent to lift me up in courage and strength.

Not long after the funeral, John Berger visited me again. He filled me in on the details of the ceremony, and I could see that tears lingered in his eyes. I felt as though John would be there as a good friend for me on the road ahead, and his mother had even written, telling me not to worry because her son would take care of me. I was beginning to see that she might be right, and I even confided this hope of his support to Mike, the hospital psychologist. I needed someone to help me navigate the sea of decisions ahead, and knowing how close Gerry and John were gave me confidence in John's advice. One of those decisions was hiring a lawyer. John investigated the crash on his own, but he also met and approved the hiring of attorney Chris Searcy to sort through the details of that fateful day.

Not long after, I met Chris Searcy for the first time. He walked to the side of my bed and in his slow Southern drawl, he said, "I'm Chris, so sorry for your loss."

Looking back into his eyes, I could see that he truly meant it. I had no memory of the accident and was desperate to know what had happened. Chris did his best to recreate that day for me from his own investigation and conversations he had with the state police. He confirmed that as the tractor-trailer drifted off the road and careened into our parked car; the car's gas tank was pushed into the rear seat and caught a spark, which caused an explosion—just as Dawn had foreseen a few days earlier.

"Judging from your burns, you were reaching into the back seat, the hottest part of the fire, as you tried to save the kids,"

Chris said. "Most likely you were driven back by the heat and smoke inhalation. Somehow, you crawled through the windshield that had shattered directly in front of you. Bystanders thought there weren't any survivors until they saw you crawling through the windshield minutes after the accident. They ran to pull you away from the car, but as soon as you realized what happened, you remembered your family and screamed, 'My life is in that car!' and you kept trying to run back into the fire to save them.

"But there was nothing you could have done, Donna." He paused and then, choked with emotion, he said, "There was nothing anyone could have done." He continued, "Eyewitnesses say the heat from the fire was so intense that they could not get too close to the car, and you were so severely burned that your skin and hair were charred. Had the windshield not blown out right in front of you, you would have been trapped and never made it out. It is a miracle you were able to get out of the car and that you are alive today."

Tears streamed down my cheeks, but I was able to ask a question I wasn't really sure I wanted answered.

"Were they in pain?"

Chris's eyes welled up, and he took a moment before he responded. "I don't know, but from the trauma, the intense heat, and the amount of smoke, they could not have been conscious for long."

I nodded and tried to control my shaky breathing. "I just keep thinking that they were scared," I said, my voice cracking as I broke down. Chris looked me in the eyes again, "I believe that in those seconds, God was holding you and your family in the palm of His hand."

I closed my eyes, squeezing the tears down my cheeks. "Lord, please take care of Gerry, Dawn, Stephen, and Michael, and tell them how much I love and miss them," I prayed silently. "And please help me because I'm not doing very well right now, and I need You to carry me because I'm not sure I can take another step."

I had reached my limit for discussing the accident. Chris left and, exhausted, I drifted off to sleep believing that Chris was yet another one of God's angel army.

As my hospital stay wore on, people continued to call and visit, including Madeline, my closest cousin and childhood best friend. I did not have any recollection of her visit, but upon hearing of it, the time and distance that had separated us melted away. Madeline and I spoke on the phone and planned out her next visit. I had too much to deal with to hold on to a grudge against anyone, particularly someone I was so close to and had shared so much life with. We realized neither one of us could remember the details of what drove a wedge between us. When Madeline returned to see me, we both cried and picked up right where we left off as best friends and confidants.

Through all the grief, I felt such comfort and peace over our reunion. The burden of our conflict was removed, and we were both lighter for it. I felt the hand of the Lord all over this reconciliation. And though the road ahead would not be easy, I knew Madeline was another angel who would always be there to lift me up.

Pain and medications left me exhausted all the time. The extended bed rest had turned my muscles to jelly, and simply walking across the room was an impossible task. I needed nurses' and therapists' assistance just to get out of bed and get through the activities of the day.

One day, several weeks into my hospital stay, I stared at my frozen hands and I wondered aloud, "Will I ever be able to play the piano again?"

Charlie, my nurse, answered, "Hmm, I don't know, were you able to play before?"

The humor was well-intentioned, but it was a serious question. The push was on for my release from the hospital, and I was undergoing a boot camp in relearning so many things we take for granted. From walking to feeding and bathing myself, there was no certainty I would be able to do anything that required strength and manual dexterity for even the most basic activities of daily living.

As my time at the hospital neared its end, my reservations about leaving all the care and assistance, to which I had become accustomed, continued to grow. My new "life," which required total care for my catastrophic injuries, was so different from my former life in Connecticut that I feared I would not be able to make the transition back home. Not only did I fear falling and undoing all the work of the multiple surgeries and therapy sessions on my hands, but I also feared returning to a new life surrounded by memories that constantly reminded me that my tomorrows had become yesterdays. I was no longer a wife, mother, or a nurse anesthetist. My hands would never recover that level of strength or dexterity needed for my profession. Truthfully, I began to panic.

The day before I was to be released, Mike, my psychologist, visited me one last time. I did not remember much of what we had said in the first few days, but I knew he was a lifeline toward hope and recovery, and I confided in him. I expressed my concerns about losing my career (which I loved), about not being able to do routine things for myself, and about never having a family again. I was in my midthirties with a carousel full of baggage and no destination.

Mike was unfazed. He looked me in the eye and said, "Donna, you will go on to add a new branch on the tree of life."

It was a phrase of comfort that I would never forget.

HEART OF
THE MATTER

When we are in the midst of a storm, we are unsure of the future, and we are constantly tempted to give in to fear and anxiety. The enemy paints everything in darkness, urging us to run, hide, fall apart, blame God, and give up our faith, while the Spirit of God softly whispers words of comfort and healing and guidance. Even if our faith is as small as a mustard seed, He will carry us through our worst tragedies. The Lord was and is a faithful presence in my life, and He will be in yours as long as He is the rock on which you stand.

Fear not, stand firm, and see the salvation of the Lord,
which He will work for you today.

—Exodus 14:13 ESV

CHAPTER 4

Where Do I Begin?

God is a shield for all those who take refuge in him.

—PSALM 18:30

F or thirty-some days, I had wanted desperately to go outside. All I could do from my hospital bed was peer out a tiny window at the sunny Florida skies and watch the palms wave at me in the breeze. I needed to feel the warmth of the sun on my face and breathe in living air so I could believe I was still alive and that the world still existed. Each time I begged to be wheeled outside, I was reminded that the risk of infection was too great. Now, after a month of yearning, I was ready to be discharged out to the world, and I could not be more terrified. My stay in the burn unit at Shands Hospital had made me weak and utterly dependent upon my isolated habitat. Icy fingers of irrational fear gripped my throat at the thought of leaving, strangling any hope that I could get into a car again, much less take care of my battered body and spirit. Room 7245, my hospital bed, and a bevy of caregivers who paraded in and out all day and night were my security and protection. How could I survive outside this cocoon? Standing and walking even the shortest distances had become a task I would not risk without the assistance of a nurse.

The first time I got out of bed was daunting. My body felt boneless, and I had been afraid the nurse was not strong enough to brace me, a task that carried grave ramifications should she have failed. One slip and fall could damage the intricate surgery performed by Dr. Siegel on my fragile hands and arms. That could mean permanent loss of function in my hands for the rest of my life. I had difficulty trusting anyone with that responsibility, myself included, especially after all I had endured.

My entire world been annihilated in the blink of an eye. I had barely survived my injuries, and I felt exposed both emotionally and physically. The staff did all they could to prepare me for my discharge, and I had gotten a little stronger. I was able to walk unassisted for short distances, but the sense of vulnerability and loss of self-confidence were overwhelming. Thoughts of leaving the hospital exacerbated those feelings and left me panicky. My mind's eye tumbled into a slideshow playing out all the horrors awaiting me between then and my arrival in Connecticut. That clip replayed continuously throughout the day. If a typical drive down the highway on a sunny Saturday afternoon could abruptly end in such tragedy, I felt that any activity, no matter how mundane, was no longer safe. My whole world had become unpredictable, and my last couple days at Shands were spent dreading the two-hour drive to Jacksonville and the flight back home.

John Berger had called days earlier and asked if I wanted him to fly down and make the trip back home with me. During his last visit, he had told me he would always be there for me, and already I was seeing that he was being true to his word. I thanked him and told him that I would like him there, but the car was already full. I was traveling with a driver, my cousin

Madeline, and a physician friend, Dr. Alberto Guinazu, who offered to make the trip back with me in case any medical issues arose. John joked that he would ride on the bumper, but despite recognizing the humor, I did not laugh. The color in life had bled out, leaving everything dreary and gray. The spectrum of my emotions had narrowed; I had forgotten how to smile, much less laugh.

When the time to leave came, the doctors gave me Valium just to get me into the car. As a result, I did not remember much of the eighty-mile drive to Jacksonville International Airport. When we arrived, Dr. Guinazu gave me more Valium for the plane ride which erased the entire trip back to Connecticut from my memory.

The drugs had worn off when we landed at New York's LaGuardia Airport, and I was too overcome with emotion to get off the plane.

"How can I have come home without my family?" I asked Madeline. "I can't do this; I can't go out there."

As people getting off the plane stared at the bandages and the tears, I felt myself drowning all over again. The plan was for me to move into Nanci and Augie's two-bedroom condo where Nanci could help me until I was able to be on my own. The beautiful dream home Gerry, the kids, and I moved into before we left for vacation was empty, and remnants of that life were relegated to brown cardboard boxes in the corner of some storage facility. Michael had been taking care of everything for me, from selling Gerry's businesses to paying household bills. I was in no condition to deal with anything but my recovery, and I was unaware of the degree to which my life was about to become consumed with intensive physical, emotional, and spiritual rehabilitation. I couldn't care for myself and working was a far-off dream. Rejoining our church community or social circles seemed daunting, and those places and people only served as painful reminders of my life with Gerry and our children. All I could do was crawl into my new life of isolation where I would live with the losses of my husband, my children, my house, my career, my social life, my body image, and my confidence. A long, hard road of "catching-up" stretched before me. Moving forward wasn't on the horizon—yet.

The first night was difficult. In the hospital everything was tailored to accommodate patients, but the real world was another story. I could not manage doorknobs, light switches, faucets, pill containers, buttons, zippers, etc. Nanci pretty much had to do everything, and as I lay exhausted in the solitude of the new and unfamiliar, my mind rattled off questions which quickly blurred into static: *Where am I? What am I doing here? Why am I alive? Where are Gerry and the children?"*

In the loneliness of my new reality, their absence was so palpable, it sucked the air out of my lungs and left me gasping. I would not have made it through that night if it wasn't for a whisper deep inside that insisted I was not alone. I clung to the same prayer.

"Lord, please take care of Gerry, Dawn, Stephen, and Michael and tell them how much I love and miss them. And please help me because I'm not doing very well right now, and I need You to carry me because I'm not sure I can take another step."

I cried until I was too exhausted to cry anymore, and then when I recovered some energy, I cried again. Sleep came in fits and starts. As soon as I felt myself dozing off, the harsh reality of my situation would startle me awake and summon more tears.

The next morning, I began what would become new full-time jobs for my sister and me. My care was all-consuming. Around 8 a.m., Nanci would come into my room to help me out of bed. First, she took off my hand splints. She helped me use the bathroom and she brushed my teeth. Then, opening and closing doors and turning on lights, she led me to the kitchen where she made breakfast for us. I used two hands to lift the coffee mug, but it still slid through my weakened fingers and spilled all over the table. Nanci promised to get paper cups "for tomorrow."

That was a funny concept. I did not think about "tomorrow" at all anymore. The pain of the present was too great to focus on the future, and even if I forced myself, what was there to focus on? All my plans had always revolved around my family, and they were buried in the past. I wasn't convinced of my healing at that point, much less moving forward—at least any time soon. Gingerly, I trusted that the Lord had a plan for me.

After breakfast, Nanci helped me back to the bathroom to get me ready for the day. We suffered through the odor that accompanied removing the skin-colored Jobst compression garments that fit like a thin wetsuit over my arms and torso. She was careful when pulling the sleeves over my hands, but even the gentlest touch still produced considerable pain. Then Nanci removed the bandages covering my hands. It felt like she was peeling off my skin one strip at a time. Even though she was gentle as she bathed me, her fingernails still scratched my burned and grafted skin and seared me with pain.

After my shower, I paused to rest against the sink while taking a long look at the person in the mirror. I still did not recognize myself. The burn scars crisscrossing my face only reflected incredible loss and the failure of a parent to protect her children. Was this the guilt that lone survivors spoke of? I stared in shock at my reflection. The skin on the right half of my nose was bright pink, and the extent to which it would heal was in doubt. My upper lip on one side was already collapsed and scarred, and I could not help but cry out, "God, look how ugly I am!" Nanci tried to comfort me, but I was haunted by the person in the mirror looking back at me. Who was I? How could I live after Gerry and our precious children endured such violent deaths? My head bowed and shoulders drooped under the weight of my grief.

Nanci then began the tedious process of applying xero-form gauze, ointments, and lotions to my face, hands, arms, shoulder, and knees. Afterward, she helped me put on clean Jobst garments, which sent electric-like shocks up my arms at every touch. Finally, she dried my hair and then we rummaged through her closet. The clothes I had taken on vacation had been burned to ashes in the car and all my clothing from home was in storage. We made do and finished up with Nanci applying layers of makeup to cover the scarring on my face. By this time, it was noon, so Nanci helped me back to the kitchen and made us lunch before we left for outpatient therapy. I had both physical and occupational therapy sessions that were so painful I had to take pain medications before they even began. Linda, my therapist, bent and flexed my swollen fingers, hands, and wrists through passive range of motion, mobilizing every joint as much as possible. The knuckles were almost completely frozen, so my fingers curved only slightly at the tips as if I was wearing thick ski gloves. She worked on my right elbow, too, because it had frozen in a contracted position like I was doing a bicep curl. Pills did little to prevent the pain.

By the time we got back, I was overcome with exhaustion. If I could have, I would have slept, but instead I sat at the kitchen table and cried. The energy I expended that day and for many days to come consumed all my strength, and the pain debilitated me, allowing unutterable grief to easily bypass any resistance I might offer. After such a long, tiring day, I didn't want to think about my family and my situation because it was too painful, but my grief was undeniable. Although the pain of my physical injuries gave me respite from my emotions, the grief never subsided; it just lay in wait to take advantage of any pause in the mental and physical realm. Like lasers of light bursting into my consciousness, I would hear little Michael calling me, see Stephen smiling, feel Dawn's hand in mine, or Gerry's arms around me as we made love that last time. Those memories tightened into a lump inside my throat, crushed my chest with their weight, and left me so lightheaded that I felt like I would lose consciousness as I sobbed. Never would I have imagined that the physical pain of grief could be so agonizing.

"Lord, please take care of Gerry, Dawn, Stephen, and Michael and tell them how much I love and miss them. And please help me because I'm not doing very well right now, and I need You to carry me because I'm not sure I can take another step."

Somehow, I managed to sleep long enough that night to have a dream. I saw Dawn standing on a playground with her long, beautiful hair in a French braid, just as she had asked me to fix it the day of the accident. "Dawnie, I miss you so much!" I cried out to her as I hugged her. She stood perfectly straight and still as she replied, "I miss you, too, Mommy." When I looked upon her face again, a solitary tear rolled down each of her cheeks.

The next night, John Berger joined Nanci, Augie, Michael, and me for dinner. Nanci was a great cook and had a knack for turning every meal into a feast, but evenings were a bad time for me. I was not interested in eating, and I could not focus on anything. It seemed I woke up each day with a measured amount of energy and no matter where I was or what I was doing, when that energy ran out, I mentally shut down. At dinner, I could not follow the conversation. John was telling a story, and I sat there staring blankly as if he were speaking in a foreign language. My mind was in a fog, numbing me to the grief and pain always knocking on the door of my consciousness. Finally, I could not even pretend to be listening anymore, and I told everyone I had to go to bed. Normally, I would have felt uncomfortable about leaving my guests, but I was devoid of feeling. My emotions were muted and dulled, and I was too exhausted to devote any energy to caring.

A few mornings later, I was in one of those rare moments of deep sleep when John burst into the bedroom. His work brought him into the area on occasion, so he stopped by with coffee and doughnuts for us.

"Get up. I brought coffee," John said.

I was mortified. I never liked seeing anybody before I was dressed, much less being covered from head to toe in burn garments. I looked like a creature out of a science-fiction movie, and here was this man in my bedroom staring at me. "No" was not a word in John's vocabulary, so completely embarrassed, I got up and had coffee with him and Nanci in my burn garments and one of Nanci's nightgowns.

We bonded over coffee and doughnuts that day. John seemed to need to talk with someone about Gerry as much as I did. It was also comforting to have him as an outlet to reminisce about the children. All my thoughts and feelings about them had been kept silent. They had become the cement holding together the fragments of my broken heart. I had no closure: no recollection of my family's death, no viewing, no funeral, and until John came by that morning, no one who could bear to talk about any of it. Nanci tried, but I knew that any mention of Gerry or the kids would reduce her to tears and quickly halt the conversation. Everyone was having a difficult time handling the loss, and the vast majority of people steered clear of any mention of it. It was as if they felt that by not mentioning Gerry or the kids, it would all go away, and I would somehow be fine. But that was not how grief worked. As a bereaved wife and mother, all I wanted to do was talk about Gerry, Dawn, Stephen, and Michael, even when it meant discussing the agony of missing them.

I felt that if I had died along with my family, it would have been so much easier for people. They could have mourned and moved on. But I didn't die. I was a constant reminder that bad things can happen to anyone, at any time. As a result, conversations with most people became awkward. People would talk about my doctor visits, my physical therapy progress, the weather, last night's dinner, and anything else that danced around the real issue that I had just lost my whole family and my life was in tatters. I continued to be in the unenviable position of feeling I needed to be strong and not express my anguish for fear of making those around me feel uncomfortable. I felt so isolated as I fought my way through constant physical and emotional pain, and this added burden only made matters even worse.

There are times of darkness when we cannot clearly hear the whisper of God's presence within us, but here was John, wanting to talk about Gerry, the kids, life, love, and loss. He was a lifeline to my sanity and emotional recovery. In retrospect, John was a God-appointed grief partner, a man of service in the angel army God had put together for me.

Somewhere among all the losses I had listed in my conversation with John, I mentioned having no clothes, so John said we would go to the mall—not tomorrow, not next week, but later that day. *Was he kidding* me?! I could *never* go to the mall the way I looked, but, again, John would not take no for an answer. He went back to work, finished his shift, and returned to pick me up a few hours later. I had to admit that getting out of the condo was a welcome break from the monotony of my days, and I got a small piece of revenge for John making me go out in public when I took him into Victoria's Secret with me to pick out underwear and pajamas. Satisfied I had enough clothing to get by, we left the mall, drove around for a while, and talked. More than anything else, it was nice to have another unfettered conversation with John. I told him about the dreams I had. I described how I had seen Gerry just after the accident, and then I told him about my dream of Dawn from a few nights before. Both dreams were so real. Simultaneously they were wonderful and cruel because they tricked me into believing, if only subconsciously and momentarily, that my precious family was still alive, only to wake to the crushing reality that they were gone from my touch.

Surprisingly, John believed that my dreams seemed so real because Gerry and the kids were not actually gone; their spirits lived on. We both believed in life after death and that my loved ones were alive with God in heaven, so maybe these dreams were comforting grace from above. Perhaps I needed to pass my dreams under the light of eternity.

John had never struck me as a particularly spiritual person, and I was curious to learn more about that side of him. Reluctantly, he began to tell me the story of his return from visiting me in the hospital. Apparently, John's girlfriend, Crystal, was unhappy that he was spending so much time investigating the accident. When he returned from Florida, she went off on a rant, saying how she missed their friend Gerry, too, and she wanted to know why John needed to visit me anyway. She wanted him home to comfort her. Her reprimand irritated John, but they got past it.

In the middle of the night, John's Rottweiler began howling, and John and Crystal awoke to the drapes blowing wildly and the vintage radiators, common in old New England homes, rattling and shaking. No windows were open, but it was as if the room had become a wind tunnel.

Crystal jumped out of bed and shouted, "Gerry's in this room, I'm getting outta here!" She grabbed her clothes and ran out of the house.

Once she was gone, the wind calmed, the rattling ceased, and the dog lay down quietly. John felt a sense of peace fall upon the room, and he went back to sleep. He never saw nor spoke to Crystal again.

HEART OF
THE MATTER

In the depths of grief, we get weary and it can be hard to envision healing. Lighten your burden by sharing your story with someone you trust. The Lord's ambassadors will listen. They will yoke themselves to you in His Name.

Come to me, all you who are weary and burdened
and I will give you rest.

—MATTHEW 11:28 NIV

CHAPTER 5

A Year of Firsts

Trust in the LORD with all your heart;
do not depend on your own understanding;
Seek his will in all you do,
and he will show you which path to take.

—Proverbs 3:5–6 NLT

D ays crawled into weeks as a steady stream of visitors filed
through my sister's condominium. Family, friends, and
acquaintances came by to show their love and support. The
children's teachers even stopped by to share their affection
for the kids and to express their anguish over such a senseless
loss. One teacher brought a word and picture autobiography
entitled *Me, Myself, and I* that Dawn had created. Reading
about my little girl in her own words both warmed my heart
and dampened my cheeks with fresh tears, but when I got to the
part about her fears, a chill ripped through me.

Dawn wrote, *I worry about my mother because I think she'll get
into a car accident*, and she had drawn a picture of a crumpled car.

Icy panic coursed through my veins as I struggled to breathe
under the wave of emotion. Dawn had never mentioned this
writing project; nor, to my knowledge, had she ever expressed
any concerns about a car accident or death. I had feared my own
death, but now I knew that Dawn had, too. However, when the
car accident occurred, I survived and everyone I loved the most

died instead. Those deaths felt worse than my own, enough to make me wish I were dead just so I could be reunited with my family. Was that desire for death what Dawn was worried about?

Part of me, or at least something inside me, had indeed died. The love I had held in my heart for my family had turned to soul-eating grief, and I was left to paint the rainbow of human emotions with a solitary color best described as "lifeless gray." It was such an overpowering transformation that I literally did not see the actual colors of life.

Autumn in Connecticut had always been my favorite season. I used to joke with the children that our colorful backyard looked like a box of Trix™ cereal, and they would chorus back, "Mom, Trix™ are for kids!" But as I looked out the window of Nanci's condo, the leaves were not green, red, yellow, or orange, and the sky was not blue. The world around me was drab and inconsequential. Nothing mattered anymore.

To be clear, I was not suicidal. I never planned or even thought of killing myself because I believed that would be a loss of trust in a God I loved and was desperately clinging to. Still, under the burden of such physical and emotional pain, I wished I were dead. I wanted to see and touch my precious family again, not when my time had come, but right at that moment. The overarching agony I endured was often unbearable, but I managed to find some solace amid the mounds of mail I collected from folks sending their condolences and prayers. It was funny how I held small yet warm and thoughtful gestures as priceless possessions. So while the simple coffee mug I had received was an ordinary cup that cost a few dollars, it meant so much more to me. The poem entitled "Footprints in the Sand" was embossed on it, and I read those beautiful words over and over again.

One night I dreamed a dream.
As I was walking along the beach with my Lord,
Across the dark sky flashed scenes from my life.
For each scene, I noticed two sets of footprints in the sand,
One belonging to me and one to my Lord.
After the last scene of my life flashed before me,
I looked back at the footprints in the sand.
I noticed that at many times along the path of my life,
especially at the very lowest and saddest times,
there was only one set of footprints.
This really troubled me, so I asked the Lord about it.
"Lord, you said once I decided to follow you,
You'd walk with me all the way.
But I noticed that during the saddest
and most troublesome times of my life,
there was only one set of footprints.
I don't understand why, when I needed You the most,
You would leave me."
He whispered, "My precious child,
I love you and will never leave you
Never, ever, during your trials and suffering.
When you saw only one set of footprints,
It was then that I carried you."[1]

When everything became overwhelming, I would look at the poem on that mug, and I would visualize God cradling me in His arms, carrying me through this perfect storm, and I would survive another day.

"Lord, please take care of Gerry, Dawn, Stephen, and Michael and tell them how much I love and miss them. And please help me because I'm not doing very well right now, and I need You to carry me because I'm not sure I can take another step."

In total, I ended up receiving over two thousand pieces of mail, and almost every single one was a pinpoint of light infused into the darkness of my grief. Still, I lived in a foggy consciousness, alternating between psychic numbness and emotional upheaval. It seemed at times I was incapable of emotional responses to even the most provoking of triggers, and then a flashback of Gerry and the kids would collapse me into a sobbing heap. All I could do was have faith that there was a bigger picture—a reason I was alive. I had to trust that the windshield breaking in front of me allowing for my escape had happened for a reason even though I found no reason left in my life. I was a single woman living in a room in someone else's home. How could I describe the absurdity of it? Nanci and Augie were more than accommodating and took wonderful care of me, but I was in emotional and psychological exile. I was trudging through a barren desert that thankfully, from time to time, offered a hopeful breeze, one that fanned the smoldering embers of my life.

In the year following the death of my loved ones, I discovered that I had a whole lot of firsts to get through. My first "first" happened to be my birthday, about a month after I left the hospital. It was awkward. People didn't know how to approach it. A jubilant "Happy Birthday!" would be misplaced, while ignoring the day all together would be equally awkward. Everyone tried their best to prepare for the big day, and I thoroughly appreciated all the warm, wonderful, well-intentioned greetings. Madeline, as always, got it right. She sent me a bouquet of flowers the morning of my birthday and wrote on the card attached to it, *I can't imagine how hard it must be to have a birthday without Gerry and the kids to celebrate with you. I am thinking of you today and want you to know that your pain is not forgotten.*

Outside of the kind greetings of my loved ones, my first "first" proved to be nothing short of a nightmare. Nanci and Michael made plans for a small group of us to go out to dinner. Coincidentally, I had an appointment that day to be fitted for a UVEX compression mask, ordered by the plastic surgeon to keep hypertrophic scarring on my face to a minimum. The mask looked and fit like a classic hockey-goalie mask, custom-molded to my face, and I was not thrilled at the prospect of yet another restrictive appliance. Jobst garments, splints, and now a mask were suffocating me, both physically and emotionally. It made me feel like I was getting sicker instead of better.

John offered to take me for the fitting that day, and as it turned out, he was just the person I needed to be my advocate. The technicians explained the process for making the mold. It was a routine procedure that was done all the time without incident, they said.

Well, not for me.

The hour-long appointment rolled into four because the technicians had applied an insufficient amount of protective barrier under the mold. As a result, instead of easily slipping off, the plaster stuck to the fragile, sensitive, newly healing skin of my face. One technician brought in another—and then another—and they all professed they had never seen this happen and were unsure how to proceed. I sat and cried while John, never one to mince words, expressed outrage for the both of us. After hours of using every technique they could conjure up to remove the now hardened mold, and then painstakingly, piece-by-piece, picking off all the plaster left embedded in my burned face, John said, "Enough!" and we left.

Already late for my birthday dinner, I was frazzled and sporting a bright pink face speckled with dots of white cement as I walked in humiliation to our table past the turning heads and startled glances of other patrons of the restaurant. As if the day had not already gone poorly enough, this restaurant was where Gerry and I had enjoyed our last dinner out together before the accident. That evoked all sorts of bittersweet memories and grief. I tried to just get through the dinner, but even the weight of the silverware became an issue. *Oh, the things we take for granted.* I discovered I did not have the strength to use the knife at all, so John had to cut my food for me. I didn't fare much better with my fork either. I would get rounds of pitying glances from around the table every time my fork clattered noisily out of my weak fingers and onto the plate. To make matters worse (if that was even possible), my poor mother in her Alzheimer's confusion sat to my left sobbing over the loss of her grandchildren. That night couldn't end soon enough.

John came back to Nanci's and we ended up conversing late into the night despite the exhaustion and absurdity of the day. It was as if John became my God-appointed pain eater. A grief partner who kept me hopeful during some of my worst times.

With days like that, I had to develop superhuman patience in healing. I had so little tolerance for it, yet there so many ways in which I needed to heal. My burn injury was complex and required an incredible amount of time, energy, and precise care to ensure a good outcome. Just when I thought I had one spot healed, a problem arose somewhere else. I was constantly trying to minimize scarring and prevent contractures that would limit my movement. Invariably, that occurred anyway, and it was back to the operating room for more surgeries.

Riding that merry-go-round was difficult. As a nurse anesthetist, I knew that the majority of my patients required follow-up care for relatively short periods of time, but burn care could go on for years. It was as if I was working double shifts at the hospital seven days a week. So many relatives and friends helped out, but after weeks and then months, the assistance tapered off. They all had families, jobs, and their own lives to live. I understood that, and I was thankful for everything everyone did for me, but I had had a family, a job, and a life to live, too. When did I sign up to give that all away? How did I end up being nothing more than a nursemaid to my disabled self? My lack of purpose was overwhelming me.

If my physical issues were like riding a merry-go-round, my emotional state was as if I was on Space Mountain. How could I grieve so many losses at once? It was just too much. In losing my children, I was no longer a mother, and in losing my husband, I was no longer a wife. I loved working, but in losing my job, I was no longer a nurse. I never even had the opportunity to say goodbye—not to my beloved family, or to all the neighbors and friends from our community, our church, the gym, the library, even from our local bakery—because I came back to a different life in a different home in a different city. There were just so many people that I came in contact within the course of a day that I would have thanked and hugged goodbye. From the garbagemen who would always go around to the side of our house when we forgot to put out the trash to the school bus drivers who protected their precious cargo as if the children were their own, I missed them all.

If I could have put all these losses into one bundle and grieved them at once, perhaps I could have organized my thoughts, but every person and activity cried out for individual recognition and created untold confusion in my mind. When I was missing my workout at the gym, I was at the peak of the roller coaster thinking, *Oh well, hopefully there will be a time when I can do that again,* but when I was missing my beautiful daughter, my heart was in my throat as the roller coaster kept dropping so low that I thought I would die. I would spend all day long on that ride until I was dizzy.

People around me were sympathetic and understanding of my plight. But, as the months wore on, I sensed "grief fatigue" in them. They had reached out to me, had worked through their own sorrow, and now they needed a change of focus. I became embarrassed and felt like a burden, because to stay in my world meant to acknowledge throughout every waking moment of every day that "bad things can happen to good people." I understood how paralyzing that could be.

On the other hand, I'm not sure people understood my need to live in the moment. I couldn't just move on, and I probably offended some in the process of declining invitations to weddings, confirmations, dinner parties, bar mitzvahs, and even family get-togethers. I just wasn't ready. With those closest to me, I never had to pretend or make excuses. But with the rest of the world, I either kept to myself or began to feign that I wasn't a sorry mess inside.

Times when I chose to stay home by myself were curiously comforting. I would sit with a cup of tea, cry, and talk to God. At times I felt He was absent, but the comfort and peace I felt in my soul when I prayed confirmed that He was not absent but perhaps closer to me than ever. That's what kept me from drowning in my own sorrow.

HEART OF
THE MATTER

A hallmark of grief is the loneliness that grips us even when we are surrounded by family and friends. The ultimate loneliness is feeling that God has abandoned us. "Where are you?" we cry out. If we are still and listen, grace calls back to us,

> Be strong and courageous . . . for it is the Lord your God who goes with you. He will not leave you or forsake you.
>
> —DEUTERONOMY 31:6 ESV

One night, as if God were answering all my petitions, I received a glimmer of hope that my struggle was not in vain. Most nights were sleepless nights. Insomnia continued to be an unwelcomed guest accompanying my grief. But on this particular night, I was able to fall into a deep sleep. In that sleep, Dawn visited me in a dream for the second time. Her hair was in the same long French braid, and I rushed over to hug her.

"Dawnie, how are you?"

"I'm fine," she replied.

"How are your brothers?" I asked, my months of anxiety turning into eagerness with each question.

"They're doing fine."

"Are you here to take care of me?"

"No, Mom," Dawn said. "My job is to help bring over little children who die. But I *am* here to make sure you find some joy in life again."

In those heartbeats between the dream state and consciousness, there could be a willing suspension of disbelief that quickly dissipates when we open our eyes to our painful reality. Even if it was only in those heartbeats, I believed it was my Dawnie I was holding in my arms. The dream felt so real that I believed I had an actual conversation with my daughter, and I studied every word and every second of my time with her. Dawn said she was making sure I found joy. What could that mean? But, more importantly, how was I to accomplish that? I needed to talk with someone about this dream, and I knew just the person I could turn to. I had learned from our conversations that John had a spiritual clarity about him that was unwavering. In relaying the dream to him, John unhesitatingly expressed his belief that this was God's grace comforting me in my darkness.

"I know it's hard," John said, "but you have to live! Gerry and the kids are expecting you to do that. You have to get better and live your life, and someday you will find joy."

As impossible as it seemed, John's confidence and conviction allowed me to begin to believe that there would be a day when I would feel better. More than that, it gave me hope-filled comfort. Surrounded on all sides by raging winds, I rested peacefully for a while in the calm eye of the storm.

John never got tired of reminiscing about Gerry and the kids, and he never ran out of stories of their escapades. Some nights I would call John after he got off his late shift and we would talk until two or three in the morning. On particularly bad nights, I would ask John to come over and sit with me so I could fall asleep. John was so supportive, but as I began to get physically stronger, depression strengthened its hold on me. I came to realize that I would need to seek professional counseling to deal with this new depth of despair.

I had never been in counseling, so I didn't know what to expect when I visited the first psychologist, a man just a little older than myself. After a few meetings, he pieced together that he was also seeing a relative of mine who was dealing with the sudden loss of his father. From there our sessions devolved into comparisons of the two losses. I was drowning in my own sorrow and had no strength, energy, or space in my heart to talk about anyone else's pain, even if it was a family member.

I moved on.

I saw an older female therapist next. She was nice enough, but she had specific topics lined up that she wanted me to talk about. I would go into a session needing to talk through a specific issue and would leave despondent over something entirely different. She was not helping me, and I began to wonder if anyone could.

My depression deepened, and after having struck out twice, I tried a Compassionate Friends Bereavement Group. At the time, this caring group did not work for me either. Everyone was a great deal older than me and no one was dealing with multiple losses, particularly of young children. With the mountain of loss overshadowing me, I wasn't ready for a group, nor did I have the necessary empathy to listen to and console others. With no success after three tries, I put my search for psychological support on hold.

Still dealing with all the firsts in my life as a widow and childless mother, the next five came in rapid-fire succession. I learned that it could be a big mistake to not plan an activity for those special days. If you had no plan, grief, like a dense fog, would roll in and swallow you up. Halloween was just twelve days before Dawn's ninth birthday, and I made a plan. John had promised that when I was ready, he would take me to the cemetery, and I thought Halloween would be a good time for that. There would be no kids' costumes, school parade, or excitement about trick-or-treating this year. Instead, I bought little pumpkins and bunches of orange and yellow flowers, and we headed up to the cemetery.

I had no idea what to expect, certainly not the carefully maintained grass that surrounded the graves. John had been anticipating the day when I would be ready and had planted grass seed. Then, depending on his schedule, he would go before or after work to tend to his grass garden. His thoughtfulness touched my heart. Together, we made arrangements for each grave out of the pumpkins and flowers I brought, and then, we stood in silence.

"Lord, please take care of Gerry, Dawn, Stephen, and Michael and tell them how much I love and miss them," I prayed in the quiet of my mind. "And please help me because I'm not doing very well right now, and I need You to carry me because I'm not sure I can take another step."

Then I cried as if my heart was being ripped in two over and over until the pieces seemed too small to split. Standing there looking at those graves made the reality of my unreality hit with unimaginable force. They were really dead. Not having seen them at any point after the crash and not being at their funeral had left open the opportunity for my mind to engage in disbelief and to think maybe this was all a bad dream that I would awake from.

When my grandparents and my dad had died, I had seen them in the casket and touched their hands. There had been no question they were gone. But this time, it was different. Until now, little taunts in the back of my mind had been able to break through and whisper, "This can't be true!" or "It's impossible!"

and at some intangible level I would actually try to convince myself of the truth in those lies. But here was proof, and in the blink of an eye, I was back to day one.

Dawn's birthday arrived next, and I had recovered sufficiently from my first visit to plan another. This time, John and I took a cheerful bouquet of Dawn's favorite purple flowers tied together with pink ribbon and a "Happy Birthday" balloon. It was less traumatic than the first visit but still crushing. Dawn was my first baby, my only girl, and we did everything together. The pain was so overwhelming, I wondered once again if I would survive.

And so it went, the first Thanksgiving, the first Christmas, and the first New Year's Eve. Mother Nature did not take into consideration that December 31 was my Stephen's seventh birthday, and she blistered Connecticut with a freezing wind. Since burn patients have trouble managing cold weather, I was not able to make the cemetery trip that I had planned for Stephen, but the tears still flowed endlessly. This time, they were for an amazing little boy who would run in from playing outside just to give me a bear hug and tell me he loved me before running back outside to continue playing. That night, I was glad that Nanci and Augie were out. I wanted to just be alone, and I decided to watch the video of the funeral that had been recorded for me.

My beloved John Borgo, the priest who had presided over my marriage to Gerry just twelve years before, led a group of seventeen priests as they concelebrated a Mass of Christian Burial for my husband and our children. There were no words to describe the feelings that overcame me as I witnessed that liturgy. Seeing the three small white caskets slowly carried in one after another, then the larger one that I knew held Gerry, sucked the air out of my lungs and forced me to my knees. I rocked and cried, but I did not turn away. The familiar strains of the hymns we sang each Sunday—the songs I had chosen—echoed a mournful peace within me, and Father Kelly's words from the Gospel of Matthew resonated.

HEART OF THE MATTER

Salvation could be lost by the wise who believe in the concept of God only in their heads. But the simple faith found in the hearts of little children embraces the personal relationship of love and trust in Him that we all need for salvation.

Jesus said: "Truly I tell you,
unless you change and become like little children,
you will never enter the kingdom of heaven.
Therefore, whoever takes the lowly position of this child
is the greatest in the kingdom of heaven.
And whoever welcomes one such child
in my name welcomes me."

—MATTHEW 18:3–5 NIV

It struck me . . . I had been forced into being a child again. No reason or logic could make sense of what had happened to me. No church, no ideology, no facts, no proof, and no explanation could adequately reconcile the concept of a loving God and the tragedy I had experienced. As a believer in Christ, I knew my hope was not in this life but in eternal salvation. I couldn't love and trust God in the good times and then reject Him in the desert of my grief. He was in that desert with me. He was caring for me, loving me, keeping me alive. Like a child, I could sob and grieve and hold on to His lifeline of promises at the same time. Simple, childlike faith was all I had left.

It would turn out to be all that I needed.

CHAPTER 6

Leaning on the Lord

Be strong and courageous. Do not be afraid;
do not be discouraged, for the LORD your God
will be with you wherever you go.

—JOSHUA 1:9

While my emotional recovery felt more like a series of setbacks, I did continue to make some progress with my physical recovery. Fed up with the UVEX mask, I opted instead for steroid injections from a plastic surgeon who specialized in facial burn injuries. Unfortunately, the pain from the lip injections made childbirth seem like a walk in the park. A human being's lips contain one of the most concentrated areas of nerve endings in the entire body, and I could not help but shake and scream in pain as the tears streamed down my face with every injection. John usually took me to those appointments because they were about an hour away, and if he didn't hold both of my hands during them, I am sure I would have reflexively smacked the syringe out of the doctor's hand. Between the sheer exhaustion of the whole ordeal and the painkillers I took beforehand, I would sleep the entire ride home. The injections seemed to be working, and the temporary agony was better than the constant discomfort of the UVEX mask.

By the end of January, I had plateaued in the occupational and physical therapy sessions for my hands, and my doctor informed me I would need more surgery. We would take the surgeries one hand at a time so that I would not completely lose functionality, although my hands were so limited that I had practically been living that way for months already. He performed multiple procedures on my left hand to increase my range of motion and dexterity. All of them included an initially painful and moderately long recovery. I waved the white flag of surrender.

The surgery went as well as could be hoped for, and, as predicted, the first week was trying. I had not gotten out much beyond doctor visits and therapy sessions before this surgery, and afterward I stayed in even more. While I was limited to one hand, I still had become much more self-sufficient than when I had first come home from Shands Hospital, so I did not need as much babysitting. I spent more time reading, answering correspondence, and helping my brother Michael as best I could with day-to-day decisions on my house and our businesses, which had not yet sold.

Amid the cold and gray of that winter, there was an ever-so-brief February thaw, and John stopped by one afternoon to take advantage of it.

"You need to get out of this house and get some fresh air," he said.

Reluctantly, I agreed, and we went for a walk. We were talking about Gerry, as we normally did, when one of the guys at the construction site whistled as we passed. John became irate even though I'm sure the construction worker would not have whistled if he had gotten a closer look at me. Still, John shouted back, and then he quickly apologized to me for losing his temper.

It caught me off guard. John had been there for me as a good friend ever since the accident. I knew he would do everything in his power to protect me from harm, but in his protectiveness

I also sensed affection, and that surprised me. John had been a God-breathed lifeline to me as I was drowning in a sea of despair, and I knew I had been leaning on him more and more, but I had not thought about us having a romantic relationship. I had all I could handle in just summoning the strength to get out of bed each day. I did not think much beyond that. Besides, John was amazing in every way. He certainly was not looking for a person like me, broken, scarred, and carrying a lifetime of baggage. I refused to allow myself to put the thoughts of John and affection together in my head, and I left it at that.

February 11 brought another tearful first. It would have been my son Michael's fourth birthday. Spike, as Nanci called him, got his nickname from the time we spiked up his hair with gel one Halloween. Nanci had called him Spike ever since. He was the easiest and sweetest little boy a mom could ever dream of. He was always getting into mischief, but he had me wrapped around his finger, and he was wrapped around my heart. Even though it was cold and icy that day, I made the trip to the cemetery with John. We put some of Michael's dinosaurs at his grave with a "Happy Birthday" balloon tied to the tail of one of them. Then we laid a single rose on each of the other graves.

Afterward, John and I went out for coffee. We sat and reminisced about Michael and his escapades, like the time he hid from Nanci, and, after frantically searching, she called the police, only to find him crouched behind the potted tree in her living room. The mood lightened after those stories, and that was when John said: "You can't stay inside that condo forever; let's go to the movies tomorrow night."

Wondering if John considered this a date and being too afraid to ask, I froze momentarily. My brain was already in enough chaos, and I was not ready to pile on yet another possibly life-changing dilemma. So I replied lightly, "You're right. I can't hide forever; I need to start doing things."

In retrospect, I should have asked what we were going to see.

The action crime thriller *Black Rain* would definitely be a movie that would interest a police officer with a ninth-degree black belt in karate, but it didn't hold much interest for me. About twenty minutes into the movie, during a particularly violent and bloody scene, I closed my eyes and put my head down, at which point John put his arm around my shoulder. The warmth of his touch sizzled through my body, making me shudder ever so slightly. From nursing training, I knew of the biological need for touch, but as much as I longed to touch and feel Gerry and the kids, I had never identified touch as one of my losses. The body often reflexively reacts before we comprehend what we are feeling, and I found myself turning toward that warmth and resting my head on John's broad shoulder. Shifting slightly in his seat, John's lips met mine and we kissed, tenderly and briefly, before he whispered, "Let's leave."

We walked in silence to the car, full of many more questions than answers, beginning with "What just happened?" John drove to a nearby church parking lot, where we stopped and talked. We discussed our feelings and concerns as well as the events of the past and visions of the future. We shared thoughts on our options, whether we were ready to move from friendship to something more and if that could ever work. We both knew that what had happened in that movie theater had the power to dramatically alter our relationship and complicate our lives. We were not a couple of kids in our twenties just starting out anymore. We were thirty-six, had both been married with children, and were aware of the difficult realities we might face.

Ultimately, we agreed to move forward. We had no guide or plan for how to navigate these uncharted waters, so we decided to trust that God had a plan for us and we would take it one day at a time. Whatever issues we could not foresee during that conversation in the parking lot, we agreed to just handle the best we could as we encountered them. John opened his heart and his home, and slowly and gingerly I stepped in. Again, I had to trust in that inner whisper that kept a flicker of hope alive in my heart and seemed to be guiding me forward.

As my injuries became less overwhelming, I found myself able to manage my pain with enough mental energy remaining to recognize the identity crisis facing me. The slate of my life had been wiped clean. Every role that had defined me was gone. I was a shattered mess, and I had no idea which piece of the puzzle to pick up first to put my life back together. The world no longer recognized me as Dawn, Stephen, and Michael's mother or Gerry's wife, although I still felt that love in my heart. While all the other hats I wore along with wife and mother were torn off that tragic day as well, "Mom" was who I was, and that was the hardest loss I faced. I simply couldn't accept that I no longer had my children to love and care for. And, no matter how I tried to reconcile it, the heartache and pain was excruciating beyond words. I became consumed with the loss of that special role that left me feeling so lost and alone.

Moving in with John helped me address the scrambled puzzle before me, and it provided the blueprint for my emotional recovery. Mindless tasks like grocery shopping, cooking simple dinners, and doing laundry were the first pieces that fit together and placed me back in familiar territory. While it was affirming to feel like a part of the world again, I still needed help in managing so many things.

One night, I decided to make Mom's famous baked chicken with potatoes and vegetables. As I was about to put the baking pan into the oven, I reflexively held it with one hand to open the oven door with the other, and underestimating the weakness of my hand, I watched in dismay as the painstakingly prepared ingredients emptied out of the pan and onto the floor. John, always ready to lend a hand, got home from work just in time to help me clean up the mess and suggest we head out for pizza instead.

Probably the most important aspect of living with John was that rather than doing things for me, he helped me do things for myself, which was exactly what I needed to feel whole again. One huge step forward was getting permission from my hand surgeon to drive. I longed for the freedom that driving provided, but my hands had not been strong enough, and ever since the accident, the roadways were like a shadow of death to me. I could not ride in a car without remembering all the anguish of the past half year, and the thought of driving terrified me.

John helped me to face that fear. He drove me to a nearby mall and parked the car. Hesitantly, I got out and walked around to the driver's side as John held the door for me, and I took my seat behind the wheel for the first time in over six months. John moved to the passenger side, and after I fastened my seat belt and let out a big sigh, he handed me the key. My hand trembled a bit as I put the key in the ignition, but John's supportive voice coaxed me into starting the car and finally driving it around that parking lot.

For several days, I practiced. We drove around town endlessly until I felt comfortable enough to go it alone. It would be a long time before I would even consider driving on the highway, but being able to run an errand or two in town was just enough independence for me to feel I was making progress.

My days were still filled with doctor visits and therapy sessions, but in the evening and on weekends, John and I slowly began to get together with relatives and friends. One couple became close friends and allies. John had introduced Tom, a friend and fellow police officer, and his wife, Jane, to Gerry and me when we were out to dinner one night the year before the crash. Jane and their three girls later had come to a birthday party at our house, and their eldest, Sarah, had even gotten together for playdates with Dawn several times. In the aftermath of the crash, Tom and Jane frequently invited John to their house, and now that John and I were together, I became part of the group. Their cozy vintage home in its quiet country setting felt safe and peaceful, and while in general it had become difficult for me to be around children, their girls' connection to Dawn, Stephen, and Michael somehow allowed me to bear the constant reminder and not feel overwhelmed.

Several times a week, Tom and Jane would invite us over. Whether it was Sunday morning breakfast or a Friday evening cookout, it helped me to remember what "normal" was as I struggled to find any sense of it in my own life.

At night, I found rest in the warmth of John's arms. As nice as spending time with family and friends was, John's love was my only respite—singular moments that grief and sadness did not permeate. He never got upset at my untimely tears, but they served as signs to me that I still had a bevy of emotions to work through. I had been putting so much on John, and as our relationship began to deepen and grow, we both recognized that I would need more support for my grief.

I was familiar with Dr. Bob Matefy from several sources over the years, but I had never met him. People described him as a sensitive and compassionate psychologist. When John suggested I give him a call, I did so without hesitation.

Dr. Matefy was tall and thin with boyishly cropped hair and an incredibly calm voice. He and I shared a love of roses, the amazingly fragrant ones you would grow in your yard. In season, he would always have a vase on the coffee table filled with his colorful, freshly cut varieties. The aroma of the rose has antidepressant properties, and I would cup my hands around the bouquet and inhale slowly and deeply as if I were breathing in peace and exhaling my grief. I would do exactly that many times in his office . . . exhale my grief one word and one tear at a time. It was safe to say that from the beginning of our first visit, I knew I had finally found a person who would be able to encourage and guide me through the difficult road ahead. Another member of God's angel army.

Bob was the one person in the world with whom I could be completely and unconditionally open. I could tell him how I was haunted by the question "Did the kids suffer?" and how much it bothered me that they died such violent deaths. The thought of those horrific injuries happening to my precious babies was too much to bear. Every time I heard a child cry out, I became panicky. Did I hear one of the kids scream? Did Gerry see the truck coming? How did I get out of the car? How long did they live? What did they feel? Could I have grabbed one of them and pulled them out? Why did it seem like time was standing still and it all happened yesterday?

Bob patiently endured these questions over and over, month after month, and calmly would remind me that the accident reports stated that nothing could have been done. He would remind me that I tried to reach back for the kids but that passengers from nearby vehicles who were forced to witness the catastrophe helped pull me through the shattered windshield and then had to restrain me when I tried to run back to the blazing car. He reminded me that memories of trauma did not follow the dictates of time, and that, as if in a time warp, survivors commonly experienced the pain and anguish just as acutely as if it had just happened. My mind could be clinging to and trying to make sense of the fleeting memories it had, so the recurrent flashback of hearing Michael screaming, seeing his desperate eyes, and watching him bring his little hands up to his face to shield himself from the merciless heat was most likely real. Those awful images were probably my last glimpse of my precious boy before he died. He was the only one I saw like that; Gerry, Stephen, and Dawn were killed on impact.

When depression ruled, which was more often than not, I wanted to scream. I knew there was a place in the recesses of my mind that stored the memories of that tragic day, but I could not access it. When I felt unexplained sadness wash over me, I knew those memories were there fueling my grief. I knew there was something I saw, heard, or did that was just beyond my mind's reach. Bob told me that this inability to recall was a protective mechanism. To survive, we sometimes put up a wall between ourselves and the horrifically painful events we had experienced. Did I want to venture beyond that wall? I had to consider whether it would change the outcome or if remembering that horror would benefit me in any way.

I reluctantly had to admit that remembering would do no good in either respect. Our scars may tell the story of where we have been, but they do not script the story of where we are headed, and I needed all my energy to write a new chapter in my life. So, with Bob's help, I would take two steps forward and one step back, inching ahead ever so slowly. Mostly, the forward steps were baby ones, and sometimes the backward steps were gigantic, but Bob helped me keep it all in perspective. Moving forward did not mean those repressed memories would be erased, just that I would make a conscious decision not to focus on them. Still, they had the power to startle me into a panic when I least expected it.

One snowy afternoon, John and I were headed home when the car started sliding and came to a stop sideways halfway down an icy hill. Instantly, terror took control, and thinking the next car down that hill would plow into us like the tractor-trailer had, I cried, jumped out of the car, and ran bootless, slipping and sliding across the street into knee-deep snow. Incidents like this always set me back to the very beginning of my grief and made me feel stuck in the past. But Bob helped me remember that I had no schedule to keep and no deadline to meet, just however long it took to learn how to cope with my inconsolable losses. Losses that truthfully would never fully be resolved this side of heaven.

As I struggled with such severe psychological and emotional distress, I also had to address the mundane and infuriating task of relearning how to use my hands. After my initial hand surgery, the lack of strength and motor control in my left hand made it feel like I was trying to do everything while wearing goalie gloves. It took me weeks, even months, to master gripping a fork again. Then, even when I got the motion down, my grasp strength would suddenly fail, and I would drop it. The exasperation did not end with utensils either. Writing, holding a cup, washing my face, putting in my contact lenses, and putting on makeup were just a few items on the long list of challenges. Failures at these tasks reminded me that my hands were in this useless state because I had been in a car accident that killed my entire family. This exacerbated my frustration and turned my relearning into an even more exhausting and, at times, depressing endeavor.

It didn't take long for me to realize there were things I simply would never be able to do again. Obviously, my work as a nurse anesthetist would be out of reach with my lack of fine motor control and grasp strength. I used to love playing classical music on the piano, but I didn't have much time for it since the children were born. With such a void in my life, I thought it would be a relaxing escape, but my efforts were cut short. My fingers no longer spanned the octave, and within a couple of minutes of playing, the arthritic-like pain in my hands was excruciating. I forced myself to accept that my piano playing days were over. And, while it tallied as yet another loss to a growing list, I saw growth and healing in my acceptance.

Whenever I recognized another loss, Bob excelled at redirecting me toward alternatives. Maybe I could not play my classical music anymore, but I could listen to it. So, John bought me a selection of Beethoven, Brahms, and Mozart to listen to throughout the day while I read, and this became my preferred form of escape. The books I became fixated on were a series entitled *Earth's Children* written by Jean M. Auel. The first book, *The Clan of Cave Bear*, was historical in the sense it involved the interaction between Neanderthals and Cro-Magnon men that actually coexisted over 18,000 years ago. The main plot revolved around Ayla, a five-year-old girl who lost her home and family in an earthquake and was left wandering in the wilderness, being ravaged by the elements, starvation, and exhaustion. I really identified with Ayla. We were both spending every minute of every day trying to merely survive, and, like her, I was starting from square one.

It was eight months after the crash and I had enough time to power through those books and many more, because I had yet another surgery, this time on the right hand. The recovery was equally as painful and arduous, but the opportunity it provided me to read and listen to my music was one positive I could take from the experience. Healing comes gradually in many forms.

Time began to weigh heavily on my heart and my spirit. Aside from the fresh surgery on my hand, the rest of my burns were healing, the injections in my lips were working, and I was gaining back the physical energy that had been sapped by weight loss and the excessive metabolic demands my body generated to heal my severe injuries. As much as I should have felt relieved, this sense of physical well-being forced open the floodgates of my emotions. My feelings had been dammed up for too long, and the levy suddenly broke. I cried for hours, completely depleting my energy and paving the way for the psychic numbness to shut down my brain. John was working, and everyone else was back to living their own lives, so my grieving was often solitary. As much as expressing this sorrow in therapy and to John was cathartic, I could not get beyond feeling unproductive and useless.

That was when an inner force led me to the next piece of the puzzle. My family had been wronged. There was an injustice to right, and I was the only person left who could do anything about it. So far, I had done nothing. Was I going to let my family down? Or was I going to do the last and only thing I could for Gerry, Dawn, Stephen, and Michael? I wanted to make a statement. I wanted to make highways safer on behalf of my family and hopefully spare even just one person from ever experiencing the torment that haunted me every day. In this way, I could channel my grief and sorrow into something meaningful.

By all accounts, I should have died in that car with my family, but I was left behind. People said it was a miracle that I survived, that there was no way I should have escaped that flaming heap of twisted metal. There had to be a reason I had been spared, and advocating for others in the name of my husband and children seemed to be the beginning of the road to understanding. Chris Searcy and I had stayed in touch throughout this time, and he was thrilled about my interest. He promised to explore the available avenues of opportunity and get back to me.

Amid all this, John and I had grown even closer, and he wanted to know if our relationship would take the next step. I could barely plan a day in advance without fearing the next catastrophe would strike, so it was overwhelming to even try to think long term. I had not yet figured out who I was. How could I be a partner to someone else? I was fearful I would not be able to fill the role of wife—or even mother—again. I was fearful I was too damaged and sad to make someone else happy. So I turned to the Lord and prayed.

"Lord, is this the right thing? Is this too soon? Am I jumping into something I'm not meant to be doing? Will I wake up in a couple of years and say what the heck am I doing here? Will he?"

I spoke with Dr. Matefy about it, and one of the things he told me was that individuals who were in happy marriages tended to be open to relationships sooner than people in unhappy marriages after losing a spouse. In other words, because I had a strong relationship with Gerry, it made sense that I was open to a relationship with John. That knowledge set me at ease about my feelings toward John, but it also concerned me. Was I considering John's marriage proposal because I had such a good marriage with Gerry or because I genuinely wanted to be with John? Complicating matters were the similarities between these two men. They had been best friends, so they had a lot of the same likes, dislikes, mannerisms, and ways of thinking and saying things. John certainly reminded me of Gerry in so many ways, and it was possible I felt strongly about him because he felt so familiar to me.

Adding to my confusion was the fact that some people did not support our relationship and were not shy about voicing their opinion. I understood that experts were proponents of waiting a year after the loss of a loved one before making irreversible decisions, and with four loved ones to mourn, I knew some of the concern for me was genuine, but some was not. For the most part, family and close friends saw John's role in my recovery firsthand and were supportive. The priest we asked to marry us had some reservations, which I respected. He had us postpone our decision until he had the chance to confer with Dr. Matefy and meet with us for several counseling sessions. But then, there were the few friends who outright told John he was making a terrible mistake. They said that he was "crazy" to tie himself down to me and all my problems, and a few others rallied behind them with underhanded whispers of our relationship being improper and disrespectful.

These issues and so many other conflicting thoughts and emotions confused and discouraged me. It took a lot of prayer and trust that God would guide me to the right decision. And as much as I wished with all my heart my acceptance was an exuberant *yes*, unfortunately, given the circumstances, it was far more restrained. An inner voice spoke to me: "John has been loving and caring from the moment God led him to the burn unit. What if this is exactly where God means for you both to be?" I didn't know where I was headed, but that message strengthened me, and I decided to go forward and pray for the best.

After making that decision, I no longer felt conflicted but peaceful and hopeful instead. Admittedly, it was an unusual way to arrive at a lifelong commitment, but I believed God was in charge, and He knew I was not ready for great joy and excitement, so peace and hope were His encouragement to sanctify our relationship in a marriage covenant.

John had been my rock for almost a year at that point. He was good for me in so many ways. Without him, I am sure I would not have survived. I knew the feelings we held for each other were genuine. To be honest, there were moments when fear would creep in and I felt unsure of myself, but I came to recognize that as my anxiety over the unpredictability of life. Fear of the next tragedy was always on my mind, especially as the one-year anniversary of the accident crept up on me.

There was a lot going on at that time, both good and not-so-good. The skin on my arms and my donor sites had healed enough that I did not have to wear the Jobst garments anymore. With John's and my wedding approaching, I was especially thankful to shed those ugly trappings, but as hopeful as I felt about my upcoming marriage, I struggled to show great excitement because I was in the middle of an ongoing war with despair. My round-the-clock job was just to chisel away another pebble from my mountain of grief, and it seemed overwhelming. My insomnia had become unbearable, and I often awoke with thoughts of the accident haunting me. Life was truly moving on all around me, but I was stuck in a place and time that dated back almost a year.

We needed a break, and my skin had healed enough for it, so John and I planned a vacation to Cape Cod. I was anxious about venturing out of my comfort zone. The Jobst garments had just come off, and not only was I worried about protecting my damaged skin from the sun but I had also grown self-conscious about my appearance. Not long before, I had been walking in town when a child spotted me and shouted, "Look, Mommy, a lady with striped legs!"

I was thirty-six years old, and I cared about my looks. Hearing I had striped legs was deflating. All this was on my mind as I prepared for a trip to the beach. It would be hot, so I would look out of place wearing pants and long sleeves, but I needed to cover my burned arms or risk my grafted skin sloughing off. I had no clue if the sand and sun would be too irritating, and if anything went wrong, I would be far removed from the help of my doctors.

Still, I desperately wanted this time for John and me. We were about to start our lives together, and this trip seemed like something that would be special for us. I did not want to start down the road of letting my fear and anxiety dictate what we did with our lives. So I took a leap of faith and went on the trip, and I was so glad I did. Thankfully, the weather was cool enough for long sleeves and shorts, and this mini vacation ended up being the first entry into the book of fond memories for John and me. It was a small but wonderful and healing step forward. We walked the beach, talked for hours, and, far away from the issues that hounded us, we laughed until we cried.

When we returned home, I became more focused on the one-year anniversary. It was important for me to give Gerry and the kids an appropriate tribute. A lot of people planned on attending, including many of Dawn and Stephen's classmates. That gave me a great deal of anxiety because I worried I would not be able to maintain my composure with all those children around.

As anticipated, the turnout was incredible. Over a hundred people joined us, including Dawn and Stephen's little friends, many of whom came up to me after the service. While I appreciated their love and support, their presence was incredibly emotional for me. I had spent months and countless trips to the cemetery preparing myself for this moment. Just when I thought I had come to peace with the tragedy and had it packed into a memory box on a shelf in the closet of my mind, my box flipped upside down, and out spilled the same questions, fears, and pain. All I could think about was how my children had missed that entire year, about how my family was dead. I could not believe it. After so much time and so many tears shed to come to terms with it, I once again could not accept the reality of their deaths, and after everyone had left, I crumpled into the emotional mess I had become accustomed to being.

The ensuing weeks were challenging. I felt I had not even begun to recover emotionally. The anniversary only served as a reminder of how much time had passed and how much further I had to go. But a developing inner strength kept propelling me forward; even when I regressed, it wouldn't take "I can't do this" for an answer.

The brightest light and blessing was that I married John and we were truly happy. It was the perfect summer day for a small justice-of-the-peace wedding in our friends' backyard while we planned a larger, more formal church wedding. I realized that in trying to reestablish who I was, there were certain parts of me that would not go away just because my family had died. Gerry was dead, but my identity as a wife remained, and I needed to love and be loved in that way. Similarly, my children were dead, but I could not give up being "Mom." I wanted more children, not just for me but also for the sake of my recent marriage to John. Mutual grief had brought us together, but I did not want tragedy to be all that bonded us. I needed a future built on joy, hope, and love, and we had just taken the first step.

John and I wanted to get pregnant right away, and, although I was in my late thirties, I didn't anticipate a problem. So when it did not happen right away, anxiety took over. Although John's and my relationship grew stronger each day, post-traumatic stress disorder (PTSD) had twisted my mind into believing that something terrible was always about to happen. I began to fear I would never have children again and that I would suddenly lose my new husband too. Every aspect of my being had changed. The happy, positive person I had been when I first married Gerry was gone, and that worried me. I lived my new life on an emotional cliff with no margin for error. Anything could push me over the edge. My fragile state would be no match for infertility. I could not bear it.

HEART OF
THE MATTER

When we are enveloped in darkness, we become fearful. At times we are confused and become panicky. At times we are paralyzed. Yet this is exactly when God wants us to let go.

At that point in my life, I was a broken mess. I was more than willing to be still and let God be God. Without knowing it, in surrendering myself and my grief to God, He was healing me from the inside out.

> Do not fear, for I am with you; do not be afraid,
> for I am your God. I will strengthen you; I will help you;
> I will hold on to you with my righteous right hand.

—ISAIAH 41:10 CSB

Perhaps that was what first prompted me to write the letter. How many times had I heard that writing down your fears and concerns could be therapeutic and free your mind and heart? So much had been going on these last few months: from the anguish of the one-year anniversary to the happy moment of our wedding, followed by the stress of surgery and trying to get pregnant. So I wrote a letter to the driver of the tractor-trailer, spilling out all my anger, outrage, and sadness. There was a hearing that Chris Searcy would be attending, and he promised to read my letter aloud in open court on my behalf. As I thought when I first met him, Chris was proving to be another angel in the army of protection that God had called together on my behalf.

As difficult as that letter was to write, when I signed my name to it, I felt a peaceful flutter in my heart. I thought about the verse from Ephesians 4:26 (ESV) that says "[D]o not let the sun go down on your anger" and realized anger could be more destructive to the person who was angry than it was to the object of that anger. Anger depleted a great deal of energy with no return on the investment, and I could not afford that. I needed to focus on my recovery. I understood there was justifiable anger and outrage that could be productive, but more often than not, when the vagaries of life rob you of that which you held precious, anger only continues to steal your life away. Anger sows seeds of bitterness in our heart that are not easy to uproot. I had to let go of the anger I felt toward the driver of the truck and the people who were responsible for his being on the road that day. It was difficult to forgive those who had not apologized for hurting me and had not asked for my forgiveness, but I knew in my heart what I had to do, and I prayed for the grace to do so. Forgiveness did not affirm nor condone the actions of the person who caused me such excruciating pain. Embracing forgiveness set my heart free from the feelings of anger and bitterness and allowed me to focus on peace, hope and, in time, joy in my life.

CHAPTER 7

Going in Circles

My health may fail, and my spirit may grow weak, but God
remains the strength of my heart; he is mine forever.

—PSALM 73:26 NLT

I exist. It was something I had to keep telling myself.
Sometimes I would look in the mirror and tentatively touch
my face. I would not recognize my reflection and I would say,
"Who are you? Are you real?" Just over a year had gone by and
I was still drowning in a sea of sorrow. John was my life raft, but
I was far from shore, treading the waters of fear and pain each
day until my body shut down and I went numb. Often, I had
to remind myself I did not die with the rest of my family, that
I had escaped the inferno inside that car, and that I had spent
a year physically recovering. My world had changed in every
way, and I felt like I had a lifetime of emotional coping ahead.

A lifetime. That was the best way to describe the accident—
as something that occurred a lifetime ago. Whenever I thought
about my life before the accident, I could only make sense of
it if I viewed it as another lifetime. I had been so violently and
abruptly cut out of my former life that the sights, sounds, touch,
and smell of it had furtively been fading from my memory with
few new experiences to replace them. I felt detached from the
world. I could function during the day, but as soon as I was not

occupied with some task, I would lose touch with reality and the darkness would envelop me.

It was just after that one-year mark that my battle-weary soul began to wonder if God was making this journey with me. I couldn't lay hold of the glory of God's presence within me, and yet, in my darkest moments, I could still sense a gentle light of hope in my heart. That was when it dawned on me. I would never break through the darkness with darkness. I needed to open the curtains a bit and begin to let the light filter in. Interestingly enough, I got some help with this from an unlikely source.

Battle Dog was a 140-pound Rottweiler, and, ironically, this midnight-black pet's glossy coat shined a ray of light into my darkness. Battle Dog was my companion when John was working, and he was a great listener. Rubbing his velvety soft ears always relaxed me and taking care of him during the day gave me something to focus on outside of myself. I did not feel so lonely with him around, and Dog, as John called him, slowly helped me appreciate humor again as only a pet's silly antics can do. More than that, loving and caring for Battle Dog gave me hope that someday I could love completely again. I knew it would take time, but I was trusting in God. I wanted to make Gerry and the kids proud of me, and I wanted John, me, and Dog to thrive.

We needed to make a fresh start; living in the house John shared with his ex-wife and daughter still held memories for him, so we decided to move. With both of us coming from families of homebuilders and mechanical contractors, we decided building our home would be a fun project we could work on together. So we bought an empty lot on a sleepy, tree-lined street and ordered a set of architectural plans out of a magazine at the hardware store for what would be our new start.

How I wished my dad were alive. He had promised to design and build a house for Gerry and me when we were ready, but, sadly, that day never came. It had been ten years since Daddy died, and I still missed him so much. The children never got to meet him, but I told them stories about my dad so often that one day Stephen, Dad's namesake, asked, "Can we take a helicopter and go see Grandpa Stephen in heaven?"

Was it silly to think they had finally met? I could always rely on my dad's love and sound advice, and I sure could have used it right then. Instead, in his absence, we borrowed a job foreman and tradesmen from my brothers' company and began the process of making all kinds of decisions in the creation of our new home. I wished I could have approached it with the excitement that a newlywed should feel when building a house with her husband, but grief often robbed me of that. My former self would have been beyond excited at the prospect of picking out flooring and finishes, choosing paint colors, and decorating a brand-new house, but at times it became a chore that I lacked the energy for. Thankfully, John was always there to lift me up.

While my nursing career was on indefinite hold because of my injured hands, motherhood was the role that could give my life meaning again. The truth was that the mother-child, husband-wife relationship did not die with death. Those roles were in my heart and in my soul, cornerstones to the foundation of what made me who I was. My family being gone did not change that, and no one would replace the part of my heart that they took with them. I had been forced to start my life over again. But just because you were thrown into the wilderness with nothing but the clothes on your back did not mean you would suddenly become a mountain woman. Rather, you would seek the comfort and shelter you were accustomed to, and that was part of what I was doing. I wanted to move forward, but in order to do so, I had to reclaim something familiar to build upon. Being a mother came naturally, and I knew that it would be a vital part of the success of my marriage to John.

We had both been self-reliant growing up. In different ways, neither of us received the full parental support we needed. We worked hard to get educated and to reach the point where we were in our lives. That self-reliance served us well in difficult times, but it could also lead us to be too independent. With all my challenges since the crash, I had no choice but to lean on John in every aspect of life. I worried about the sustainability of that sort of relationship. I felt we needed something else to connect us, because I could see how delicate the relationship between two very independent people could be. I stressed to John, "We need a bond."

Even as I said those words, they haunted me with the guilt of feeling I was somehow betraying Gerry, Dawn, Stephen, and Michael by expressing my love and desire for a future with John. I knew that I was not abandoning them, but it still haunted me. It was so hard to focus on the pinpoint of light within me when I was shrouded in darkness, but there could be no greater way for me to fully commit my fragile heart to John than through our child. I had experienced that miracle three times over with Gerry, and I knew how incredibly precious it was. I wanted us to add that new branch on the tree of life.

With the months passing and the disappointment of not getting pregnant mounting, my grief intensified. In the reading

I had done on the subject, I learned that we attached our hopes, dreams, and expectations to each child's birth. They carried our lineage in their genes, and in many ways our future. So when a child died, parents felt like their future and immortality died, too. I certainly felt that, and with each failed attempt to conceive, I felt it more deeply.

After being unable to get pregnant naturally, my doctor at Yale New Haven Hospital prescribed a fertility drug. While it would take a while to work, it took no time for me to develop some unpleasant side effects including a splitting, unrelenting headache. Still, I took encouragement in knowing that I was that much closer to becoming a mother again, so I was willing to bear the awful pain.

A year had passed, and I spent a great deal of time in Bob's office discussing infertility and cumulative grief. While I was making some progress in my emotional recovery, it was as if the tragedy loomed over me, casting a shadow that always threatened to overtake my thoughts. As Bob put it, "Life was full of emotional landmines."

That was another reason John and I wanted to move. Bridgeport was where John and I grew up. We had large extended networks of acquaintances and friends there. Every time we ventured out, we invariably ran into someone we knew. This usually led to well-meaning but awkward exchanges where people were unsure about whether or not to bring up my loss. In his book *A Grief Observed*, C.S. Lewis said it best, "I hate it when they do, and if they don't." We needed time to heal away from the landmines.[1]

Situations like this would often come up in my sessions with Bob. I would tell him things like "The memories never vanish.

They just get stuffed from one side of the mind to another" or "I just can't adjust to my kids not growing up and having their own children. How can I think long term? When John tells me he'll protect me, I tell him that life no longer feels predictable to me. My biggest fear about being married and starting a new family is that something terrible will happen again."

Then I would inhale the fragrant roses Bob kept on his coffee table and do my best to exhale my sadness. That alone rarely worked, but Bob always seemed to find a way to help me feel the tiniest bit better about things. Whenever I visited him, I managed to at least take baby steps forward, and the countless tears I spilled in his office eroded away countless pebbles from my mountain of grief.

Sadly, it was not long before another member of my family had to make an appointment at Yale. My mother's Alzheimer's disease had progressed. Much like with my attempts at getting pregnant, none of the doctors at Yale had a "cure" for Mom, so my siblings and I gradually assumed responsibility for her well-being.

Taking care of my mother and her household served as another way to distract myself from my grief. That act of putting another person's interests ahead of my own had thera-peutic value for me. Still, it was difficult to see my mother get progressively worse each week. I had already lost my father and "Mom," and now I was watching my mother slowly fade. In time, she would no longer remember who I was—or even who *she* was—which made me even sadder.

Out of the dark cloud of my grief, a silver lining shone through that November. While we were married in a civil ceremony two months prior, it did not compare to the grace and beauty of our church wedding. If John's and my traditional church wedding day was a harbinger of life to come, we were off to a truly blessed start. It was a beautiful fall day in New England: an unusually sunny seventy-five degrees with an abundance of the colorful leaves of fall still clinging to the trees. Yes, there was healing in my ability to see color again. Forty family members and friends joined us as John and I exchanged vows. At the reception we greeted our family and guests with the soft, sweet notes of a three-piece chamber group serenading us in the background. Gaily decorated in pink-and-white candles, flowers, balloons, and ribbons, a joy and happiness filled the room, undisturbed by sadness or grief. It was as if Gerry, Dawn, Stephen, and Michael were celebrating with us, and they would not let their physical absence distract from the day.

HEART OF THE MATTER

The only way to survive grief is to step away from it from time to time.[2] On any given workday, there is a lunch break and a couple of coffee breaks. Grief is hard work, and we deserve regular breaks from it as well. We need breaks to regain our strength and endurance. Whether it's resting, reading, gardening, or spending a day with your grandchild, take a break. It will help you heal.

This is what the Lord, the God of your ancestor David, says:
"I have heard your prayer and seen your tears.
I will heal you . . ."

—2 Kings 20:5 NIV

Unfortunately, our happiness was dampened as the fertility drug failed, perpetuating the pattern of two steps forward and one giant step backward. Another month wore on and we experienced another failure. It was a difficult few months with my birthday, Halloween, Dawn's birthday, and Thanksgiving having passed. Christmas, New Year's Eve, and Stephen's birthday were on the horizon. The continued infertility dealt a double blow. Each failed attempt at getting pregnant had me despondent over not only my infertility but also my many losses. Then, with all the energy and effort I was putting into getting pregnant, I still could not help but feel somehow disloyal to the children I was desperately missing.

Just when I needed someone who could truly empathize, another ray of light filtered into my life. A woman who had lost her two sons in a car accident in Florida reached out to me. Two years prior to the crash that killed Gerry and our children, a driver ran a stop sign and broadsided Debbie Thompson's vehicle, seriously injuring her and killing her two sons, Liam and Lenny, ages twelve and thirteen. When Debbie and her husband, Doug, met John and me, she shared the details of her grief journey and provided encouragement that I could someday be less fearful and live life more fully. Just as importantly, she gave me hope for having more children. About seven months after her crash, Debbie had become pregnant, and she and Doug now had a young son named Noah. I could see how important the role of "mom" was to Debbie and how Noah did not replace Liam and Lenny nor diminish her love for them. Debbie still carried around their pictures in her purse and showed them as lovingly to me as she did those of her newborn child. Instead of seeing a divide between their new son and their deceased children, I saw how Debbie, Doug, and Noah together created a new branch on that tree of life in much the same way that John and I hoped to do. Debbie's example, along with that whisper inside, told me I could do this. It would not be easy, but it was possible.

Debbie and I became friends, and she became an invaluable resource, even connecting me with a support group called "Alive Alone." Alive Alone was a group of bereaved parents who had no surviving children. Kay and Rodney Bevington created this network after their beloved daughter and only child, Rhonda, died unexpectedly from complications after surgery. They compiled a quarterly newsletter made up of tributes, pictures, and poems from grieving parents and personally responded to everyone who contacted them. I read my first newsletter, and it was like being in a group of close friends who truly shared what I was going through. I sobbed over each entry as I read about so many tragic losses, but I was relieved to know I was neither crazy nor alone in my grief.

Still, gloom and doom often engulfed me. With less frequent doctor appointments to deal with, distractions from my grief continued to decline while reminders rushed in to take their place. Grief had become so private to me that I felt insecure displaying it except while sitting alone in my room. I was self-conscious about sharing it with anyone other than John and Bob, but I had reached a point where I could no longer control it. To be the person crying in public that everyone would stare at and wonder about was embarrassing, but on occasion my sorrow would just spill out.

One night as we sat in a new restaurant sipping wine and reading our menus, I suddenly burst into tears. There was no specific reason for it other than my grief had reached volcanic proportions that I could no longer contain.

"What's the matter?" John asked.

"I don't know," I said, continuing to sob.

John sat perplexed for a moment. He looked around the restaurant in bewilderment at all the people who likely had directed their attention toward us. My eyes were too clouded with tears to see, and I was too consumed with sadness to care what anyone else thought.

"Do you want to leave?"

"No."

"So you want to stay and order dinner?" John asked incredulously. I shook my head yes.

John paused. Then he leaned in. "What can I do to help?"

I continued to cry into the napkin I held in my hands. Without offering John anything he could do to help me other than to stay at the restaurant, he reluctantly turned back to his menu.

Shortly afterward, the waiter arrived to take our order.

"I think we might need a minute," John said, nodding at me crying across the table. The waiter took the cue and hurried away.

John had to deal with so many moments like that. My depression had just grown so overwhelming that I could not escape it. Worse yet, the flashbacks grew ever more frequent and crippling as the memories of the trauma started to filter through the cracks. Whenever I would hear a child scream, I would feel panicky.

One night, I was awakened with a powerful jolt that I believed was a memory of the moment of impact. I had discussed this with Dr. Matefy. No good could come from me remembering these horrors, and now I feared it would all come flooding back and wash me away. I knew I needed to find peace or going forward would be impossible. But all the pain and feelings were *so* visceral. When I could briefly clear my mind, something like interacting with a friend's child would catch me off guard and make coping with the grief that much more difficult. I would go home and sob.

Throughout this time I continued to work with Chris Searcy and the wonderful people in his law firm in to make sense of what had happened and to memorialize my family in a meaningful way. As the particulars of the crash continued to be uncovered, the specifics of how Gerry and the children died made their loss even more devastating. For a long time, I was reeling from the fact that they were dead, so I did not ask for a lot of information. John and Chris also tried to shield me from the gruesome details, but with my background in nursing, I knew the questions to ask when I was ready. Eventually, I came to know the paralyzing truth that in addition to the smoke inhalation and horrific burns, the husband and children I loved so deeply suffered catastrophic head, neck, and chest injuries. I was distraught because the question "Did Gerry and the kids suffer?" still haunted me, and here was proof of even more trauma they had sustained. They died such horribly violent deaths, but were they aware of what was happening? I prayed that they were not aware and that they did not suffer, but still the question echoed like a scream in a canyon. I wanted to continue to contribute to the investigation, but the repeated questioning and depositions proved to be exhausting, another burden that weighed me down.

As the new year approached, things did not begin to look any better. John's father was ready to retire, and John devoted a lot of time to dissolving the company. Meanwhile, we were building our house in Fairfield and trying to plan our family. Unfortunately, the fertility drug trials were not any help in that regard. After four or five attempts, the doctors conceded that it seemed unlikely to work, so they suggested we switch medications and try a new course. Our chances of getting pregnant with this new regimen were significantly better, they explained. I wanted to scream at them: "Why did we just waste months on something that was less likely to work?"

It was a crushing blow to John and me. We were both defeated by the cycle of anticipation and disappointment. I was in my late thirties and the clock was ticking. Beyond that, I was frustrated with the uninspired cookie-cutter approach of my doctors.

We left the office that day more frustrated than hopeful over the prospects of a new procedure, but my spirit was soon refreshed by another dream. There had been several dreams about Dawn up to this point, but I had my first dream about Michael one winter night. In the dream, his teacher called and asked me to pick him up because he would not speak to anyone. When I got to Michael's school, I rushed over and put my arms around him. I did not remember what was said, if anything, but I will never forget the sensation. I could feel him. I could actually feel his smooth, soft cheek against mine. I smelled him, and he smelled like my baby boy.

When I woke up, I was completely confused but not sad. I was so excited that I told not only John about my dream but also Dr. Matefy. Since I had gotten to know and trust him, I hoped his knowledge of psychology would help me gain a better understanding of the memories outside of my awareness that hovered around me. With his help, I came to understand that we are created so wonderfully that even when we sleep, we can heal our minds and bodies. Dreams of my loved ones served to comfort me and assure me that they were okay. They also helped me to resolve my guilt. In my situation, surviving and not being able to protect my children was a tremendous burden to carry. No matter how many times countless people told me there was nothing I could have done, I still felt I should have done *something*. This dream seemed to say, "Mom, don't worry, I'm okay," and it made me think of the lines of a poem by James Lowell that a friend had sent me.

> Immortal? I feel it and I know it,
> Who doubts it of such as [he]?
> But that is the pang's very secret,—
> Immortal away from me.
> Communion in spirit! Forgive me,
> But I, who am earthly and weak,
> Would give all my incomes from dreamland
> For a touch of [his] hand on my cheek.[3]

Was this a gift? A touch on my cheek? Was that inner voice comforting me and telling me they were okay? I believed I would see my family again and that a future existed beyond the gloomy clouds hanging over my head. I wished this glimmer of hope would stoke the smoldering embers of my heart back to abundant life. That inner voice gave me hope that I was headed in the right direction. I wasn't walking on my own yet, but some mighty arms had claimed me—Jesus was carrying me forward through it all.

HEART OF
THE MATTER

By now it is evident that on the journey through grief, we don't always move forward. It is more like a trek up a very long spiral staircase. We make what feels like imperceptible progress and, in those spirals, we keep encountering the same feelings and emotions. We pull ourselves together, we sob uncontrollably. There is a day of calm, then a day of panic. "This really happened," we tell ourselves, only to follow up with "This could not have happened." Gaining resolve, we say: "I can do this." Moments later, we crumble, saying, "I can't do this." We may not realize it at the time, but Jesus is deep in those spirals with us. And as we go round and round, He makes sure that each step leads us forward.

Trust in the Lord with all your heart, and do not lean on your
own understanding. In all your ways acknowledge Him,
and He will make straight your paths.

—Proverbs 3:5–6 ESV

CHAPTER 8

Dark Night of the Soul

"For I know the plans I have for you," declares the LORD,
"plans to prosper you and not to harm you,
plans to give you hope and a future."

—JEREMIAH 29:11 NIV

Winter in New England was bitterly cold. As I stood on the sidewalk in Manhattan waiting to cross the street, the frigid wind whipped my nose and cheeks. I wrapped my coat tighter across my chest and tucked my chin into the collar to shield my face, which already stung with the cold. My fingers were numb despite my gloves. They were all the typical symptoms I experienced with my burned and grafted skin in this weather, and I knew they would only worsen. I needed to get out of the cold, but there never seemed to be a break in traffic.

If not for the recent excitement over my potential pregnancy, the pain and threat of permanent damage to my skin may have caused me to become anxious and scared. Instead, there was joy in my heart for the first time since the accident. John and I thought that I might be pregnant. Nothing in the world could make me happier.

The cars sped past, bouncing and banging along the potholes and dips in the battered city street. My former self may have considered making a run for it between cars, but I was much more cautious now.

Finally, my patience paid off as a tall, broad-shouldered man with auburn hair crossed the street toward me. As he approached, I figured it was safe, so I crossed using the stranger passing by me as a shield. We each made it to the other side of the street, but when I turned to John, I discovered he was still stuck on the opposite side of the street with the traffic whizzing. When John finally caught up to me, he was frantic.

"Are you crazy?" he barked. "Running out in the street like that, you could've been killed!"

I was confused. Since the accident, I had become hypervigilant. I would never carelessly dart into oncoming traffic.

"What? What are you talking about? I crossed with that guy."

"What guy?" John asked.

"The guy that passed by me. The big, tall guy with kind of reddish hair. He was walking up the street from me, blocking all the traffic."

John's face went pale. "Donna," he said, "there wasn't anyone there."

I laughed. "John, yes there was. He walked right by me."

John shook his head. "No, there wasn't. I was watching you the entire time and there was never anyone next to you."

How could that be? I looked across the street to try to spot the tall man with the auburn hair, but he was gone. So, embarrassed and with no way to prove his existence to John, I shrugged, and we continued on our way.

For some reason, that man stuck in my mind. Something about the whole exchange comforted me. That man had protected me from what was mortal danger in John's eyes, and then, he just vanished into the crowd, like a guardian angel that appeared when needed and then faded into the periphery. I felt safe and protected, like my steps were being led along a path of purpose, which caused me to await my pregnancy test result with even more excitement. I just *knew* that I was pregnant.

That afternoon, the phone rang, and I rushed to answer it with the joy in my heart swelling in anticipation. When I heard my doctor's voice, my heart sank, and I collapsed down on my bed. The intermittent excitement that had been propelling me for months dealt yet another cruel blow.

That loss of hope and the consequent lack of desire to go on swallowed me up. I was drowning again. I felt like my heart was ripped from my chest. It was pain—actual, physical pain. My hands started shaking, and I felt jittery, panicky, like something awful had just happened. My mind teleported me back to the scene of the crash. I wanted to run away from it all, but there was nowhere to go. I was trapped inside my head. I could not process anything except panic and terror. I kept thinking I had to get a grip, but then I thought of Gerry and the kids. God, I missed them. I wanted them back.

I wanted them *back*!

Why did this happen? I was trying so hard to go on, but I was paralyzed. Bitter.

"Lord, please take care of Gerry, Dawn, Stephen, and Michael and tell them how much I love and miss them. And please help me because I'm not doing very well right now, and I need You to carry me because I'm not sure I can take another step."

Life seemed meaningless and I hadn't heard the answer to my prayers that I was looking for in a year and a half. There had to be some reason why my three children were torn away from me, and I could not have another. What was I missing? All my life it seemed I had only been able to rely on one person—me— and now I had let myself down and there was no one to pick me back up. I felt abandoned. *Where are You, God?* This was a cup of inky darkness that had been percolating for a while.

It was the only thought that echoed in my head. There was no God. My hope had turned to despair, and I felt myself being sucked into a black abyss. I could not hold on any longer, and, like grains of sand sifting through my fingers, I felt myself and my faith slipping away. "There is no God," I sobbed. I tumbled further into darkness, into nothingness, into meaninglessness, until I fell across the bed in a catatonic-like state—thinking, hearing, and seeing nothing.

HEART OF THE MATTER

Something has happened, and nothing makes sense anymore. Our sense of purpose has collapsed and ushered us into a state of meaninglessness. We have entered the "dark night of the soul."[1] A spiritual death of self, followed by rebirth. Lost in a vacuum of inky darkness, my senses completely shut down. In that void, the love of God broke through my sorrow and despair. Initially, I was scared and filled with trepidation, but after wandering through the desolate wilderness, I found myself transformed. My life had meaning again. Not the meaning that my mind or the world around me created but the real meaning that God intended. Embracing it made all the difference in healing and being able to move forward.

In the dark night of the soul, bright flows the river of God.

—St. John of the Cross, "Dark Night of the Soul"[2]

I'm not sure how long it was before I became aware of my surroundings again. Nor did I have any recollection of what trans-
pired during that time, other than feeling as if I were free-falling
in a completely black, dreamless sleep. As I slowly emerged
out of that darkness, I became aware it was still daytime. The
late afternoon sun poured through the bedroom window, and
I realized my heart was full of an inexplicable sense of peace
and calm. When I became fully awake, a quiet acceptance
had washed away my despair. This acceptance did not feel like
a heartbreaking defeat but rather a complete surrender of control over myself and the circumstances of my life to God.

In that blackness, I believe that the Lord wasn't focused
on the words coming out of my mouth; He was listening and
responding to the groans of my heart. Our feelings are not
always trustworthy, but God is. In that silent blackness, He
was not absent; He was working things together for my good,
according to His purposes. Gut-wrenching remorse washed over
me for denying a God who was always providing for me, who
was always watching over me, and I begged for His forgiveness.

"Lord, I am so sorry for doubting You. You *are* my Lord
and Savior, and I promise I will never doubt Your presence in
my life again."

It was at this lowest point I realized that faith was not
a collection of intangible thoughts. The grace that enabled faith
was a gift from God, a strength that led our thoughts, words,
and actions to give Him glory. The grace that enabled faith
in the Lord and His Word was a gift to be thankful for, a gift
to embrace, a gift that brought joy in all seasons. Living a life

of faith could be difficult, but, for me, to live without it was impossible. For that brief moment, I had tasted death with no hope of salvation. I knew I would never again drink from that cup of denial. I would never again question the gift of grace that I realized and embraced in the "dark night of my soul."

I had been confused. There were times I felt that God had abandoned me, but through it all He was closer than ever, creating a new heart of surrender in me. I believe in that ink-black darkness, I was presented with two choices: I could continue to live in the shadow of grief and despair and lose myself down a self-destructive path. Or I could take the Hand of God that was reaching out to me and fully surrender myself and my losses over to Him. More than ever before, I felt the desire to seek Him out and abide in Him.

In doing so, I had to entertain the idea I may not be able to get pregnant. I wanted children so badly, but maybe that was not God's plan for John and me. Waiting for an answer was almost unbearable, and the many tears I spilled were beyond endurance. Even though I was a mess, John's love was unconditional, and he was always there for me. I thought we needed the bond of children to get through our grief and for me to put the pieces back together. But it gradually became clear to me that even without having any children together, I loved John as unconditionally as he loved me, and we were fully committed to one another.

What a paradoxical concept to grasp. I had a wonderful marriage to Gerry for twelve years, and then I woke up one day to find that I was married to someone else. Gerry and I never had some big falling out that left me with any negative feelings toward him, as can be the case in a breakup or divorce.

At the moment we were torn apart, I loved Gerry dearly, and it was difficult to reconcile how I could love another man as my husband. It took reflecting on my children to be able to understand it. I remembered the revelation when I was pregnant with Stephen and burst into tears while rocking Dawn to sleep. I thought I was about to lose my special relationship with her. I thought I would not have any room in my heart to love Stephen as much as I loved Dawn, but when Stephen came, I found that my fears were unfounded. I may have had to divide my time, but I was able to multiply my love, and my heart embraced them both effortlessly.

That was how it was with Gerry and John. I loved Gerry with all my heart, and I never stopped loving him. In my marriage to John, the intense challenges that we faced together forged deep roots of enduring love. I loved John for the steadfast person he was and for being able to make me laugh even in the worst of circumstances. When people stared at my scars and I felt self-conscious in public, John would throw his arm around my shoulder and whisper, "It's okay, you're my little french fry."

John was such a french fry aficionado that I could not help but smile at that quip. He always had a way of casting light into my darkness.

Maybe that was the key to drawing closer to God. Jesus had given us two main directives: "Love . . . God and love your neighbor as yourself" (Mark 12:30–31). I felt closer to God than ever, and my love for John was proof that after all the pain and grief, my heart was not broken and destroyed forever; it still could love. It was possible that having more children might not be in God's plan for us. But if I was capable of opening my heart to John, I could do the same for people who were hurting like me. People who needed someone who could understand their grief and pain. It would not be easy, but sharing my story and reaching out to people in need was something I felt I had to do. I had been on the receiving end of "love thy neighbor" for a while. It was time to embrace the giving end, and I was uniquely suited for it. As Henri Nouwen wrote in his book *The Wounded Healer*, "[O]ur service will not be perceived as authentic unless it comes from a heart wounded by the suffering about which we speak."[3]

As it turned out, it was not long before one such opportunity presented itself. Just after John and I moved into our traditional white colonial home with its red-brick accents and grassy yard, I received a call from a nurse at Yale New Haven Hospital. There had been a house fire in western Connecticut, and a father and his three children were killed. Only the mother, Heather, and one daughter survived. The nurse knew of my accident and wanted to know if I would be willing to speak with Heather.

I surprised myself with my immediate response of "Yes, of course." Grieving was such a solitary process, and there was no benevolence in it. But a little bit of the old me seemed to make an appearance in that unfettered response. Still, when a tragedy made the world around us unpredictable, a significant loss of confidence accompanied it, and once I hung up, the insecure me immediately began a self-interrogation.

"Can I do this? What will I say? I have so much of my own sorrow, how will I be able to help her?"

In response to these questions, there was an inner strength that calmed my heart. "You can do this," I told myself. I remembered reading that often the test of courage is not to die but to live.[4] I needed to take that first step out of my selfness. I needed to prove I was living.

Heather and I spoke several times, and I invited her and her daughter to come visit. It was not an easy meeting. Heather was as inconsolable as I had been at that time during my grief journey. I did not feel like I was able to be much help, but in being a little bit further along, I was hopeful that I was at least a pinpoint of light in her darkness, as so many people had been for me.

Another point of light for me turned out to be a friend who I learned had lost a child many years before. Liz was in her fifties with grown children, and she asked me to join her for lunch one day where she revealed that her four-year-old daughter had drowned in the river that coursed through her backyard. She detailed the pain and guilt that consumed her after losing her daughter and she spoke of the time, energy, and courage required to deal with her mountain of grief. After three years, she felt the cloud had finally lifted and she was able to feel whole and healthy again.

Still grasping at any promise of less onerous healing, I took the concept that grief possibly had an expiration date to heart. It gave me a goal to focus on and a promise that I would not always feel like I felt that day. I did not have to hang on so tightly to the past or work so hard to rein in the future. I needed to replace my anxiety with patience and stillness. This idea of an end goal was important for me because I still was dealing with moments of debilitating depression. In reaching out to Heather, I realized not only how far I had come but also how far I still had to go.

Despite my renewed dedication to my faith, going back to church did not seem to help. I felt isolated and disconnected. Well- intentioned homilies did not reach the special needs of my soul at that time. Church cried out "family" to me and pulled me back into a time gone by. God and I needed alone time to forge an enduring relationship out of His Word and

His grace and my surrender. This made John 15:4 come to my mind. "Abide in me, and I in you. The branch cannot bear fruit by itself, unless it abides in the vine. Neither can you, unless you abide in me."

For me, the word "abide" meant more than live, remain, or stay. It also meant to surrender myself and rest in Him. The vine became a cocoon of sorts that nurtured the close, personal relationship with the Lord that I needed and wanted. It was there I found rest and the grace that would enable me to bear fruit again.

I couldn't remember what happened during the accident, but my mind had a way of fabricating images from the information that had been relayed to me, and it would not stop. I was constantly going back to the same questions, back to my children. Did they know what happened? Were they in pain? Did they cry out for me? I was their mother, and it was my job to protect them, but after two years and countless attempts to convince myself, I finally came to accept that there was nothing I could have done. Yet this time warp of repetitive thought patterns put the brakes on my healing. I needed an exit strategy.

All this grief was compounded by the fact that after what seemed to be endless months of infertility, we decided to get a second opinion. John and I were shocked to hear that our best option was in vitro fertilization (IVF). That had been our best option from the very beginning, and we were devastated and angry to think that we had pointlessly wasted our time, energy, and resources.

I again had to consider the rapidly increasing possibility that God had a future for me that did not include children, but

I had this feeling He didn't want me to stop trying just yet. An inner voice led me to continue forward rather than give up. It was hard work cultivating the positive and focusing on hope and trust, but grace has the power to propel us forward.

IVF had definite physical, spiritual, emotional, moral, and ethical considerations that called for careful consideration. We discussed it with Father Mike, who officiated at our wedding. He told us that after what we had been through, it was difficult for him to discourage us from exploring this option. He summed it up so perfectly: "If God chooses to bless you with a child through this process, we will celebrate new life, and we will love and welcome that child into our community of faith."

With that blessing we decided to take the final step in infertility—IVF. The thought that we were approaching the last exit on the highway was terrifying. If I did not get pregnant, I would have to consider a new direction for my life, and I simply was not sure I was ready to face that. I had faith and trust in God, but I was weak and easily overwhelmed. The thought of losing this hope of motherhood and starting in a new direction panicked me. I prayed for guidance and kept busy finalizing the details of our new house, caring for my mom, and helping John with his father's business, while we explored the options of IVF. Although it had an overall success rate of 30 percent, I could only focus on the 70 percent failure rate.

With limited confidence but trust that God was beside us, John and I went forward with our first IVF cycle. The months of injections, extreme hormonal changes, myriad appointments for ultrasounds, blood draws, and egg harvesting, which culminated in the embryo transfer, were exhausting. Then, after all that, the only outcome was those sterile words: "I'm sorry, but this cycle was not successful."

The words cut like a knife. I lost the struggle deep inside of me to protect and nurture our baby. Our child had died. It was devastating, and while we comforted each other over this loss in the ensuing days, I was forced to face some really difficult truths. Before the accident, I asked God to lead me to be the best possible person for myself and my family. I never dreamed He would call on me to bear such pain. This tragedy was the biggest test of my faith. When the tears flowed, the voice in my head was saying, "I don't want to be here. I want to be with them. I don't belong here. My family is together with God and I belong with them."

It was difficult to stand strong under the burden of my loss. On the outside I may have looked okay, but the dizzying array of thoughts in my head never stopped sapping my energy. Exactly what kept me going was somewhat of a puzzle. When someone asked me that question, I felt strong in saying that I was waiting on a plan that God had for me and that God placed John in my life to wait with me. But at my lowest points, I reverted back to "Why did this happen? Why isn't it the way it used to be? Why am I putting myself through all this? Why am I alive?" It would have been so much easier and far less painful if I had died too.

"How long does it take to rebuild thirty-five years?" I sometimes wondered aloud. "Can I ever do it?" I would come to learn that living is not about rebuilding the past, it is about using the past as the cornerstone upon which we build the future.

In reflecting on those years, I realized my grief was like the ocean on a windy day: A cavalcade of endless waves. My optimism would crest, and then I would inevitably recede into the trough of depression. I needed to learn emotionally how to do more sailing and less rowing across this cycle of extremes.

John and I decided to take a break from IVF. It was the first Christmas in our new home, and Laura would be coming for her one-week visit. During this past year, family and friends had continued to be a support to John and me, and we thought hosting them all at a home of our own this Christmas would be a happy first for us. So we focused our energy and attention on decorating for the holiday. We dusted off boxes with ornaments and lights that had been in storage for two years and picked out a freshly cut Douglas fir tree. We would celebrate life and faith together and create new traditions and memories, but that did not mean we forgot Gerry and the kids. As part of our preparations, we trekked up to the cemetery with gaily decorated wreaths, one for each snow-covered grave. It was a beautiful peace-filled Christmas. Another milestone in healing, another step in moving forward. John and I got through the holidays with less sadness and more hope than ever before.

Winter ended with two more months of infertility crashing me into another trough of depression. Dr. Matefy had discussed the effects of PTSD with me, and I agreed to see a specialist for it.

Dr. Judianne Denson-Gerber was a psychiatrist who specialized in areas such as PTSD. She was somewhat disheveled, colorfully dressed, had a nest of gray hair perched on top of her head, and made quite the impression as she chatted and shuffled around the room.

When Dr. Denson-Gerber began her first session with me, I discovered that her demeanor could not be more contrary to my initial impression. She was prepared and diligent, having already reviewed all my files and having spoken with John, some of my family members, and a few close friends. Moreover,

I could tell her heart was breaking with mine. Judi was the most caring, empathetic person I ever had met. We talked a lot about my past, beginning with my childhood. She asked about Mom and my parents and was disturbed to hear about some of the ways Mom had disciplined me. We discussed Gerry, the kids, and our family life. I told her how terrified I still was of the burn unit, how I would rather die than have to relive that horror.

We eventually made it all the way up to (what was then) present day, and I shared my heartache over my most recent IVF failure. I cried and told her how ugly I thought my scars were and how my life was without meaning. I knew in my heart God would take care of me, that He was just as sad as I was, but in my weak "humanness," at times I felt like I wasn't making any progress in my healing.

After spending the bulk of the time listening and sympathizing, Judi began speaking, and I learned how truly brilliant she was. She explained the symptoms of PTSD, and after recognizing I had all the symptoms—intrusive memories, avoidance, negative changes in thinking and mood, and changes in emotional reactions—I was relieved to feel not so unhinged anymore. Judi said she believed I was one of the best-adjusted survivors of child abuse she had ever met. Still, I did have chronic and reactivated PTSD that dated all the way back to the physical and emotional abuse I had suffered as a child. I had put all that pain "on a shelf," as Judi described it, and I had made restitution for it by committing to be a mother who provided the most loving, warm childhood for my kids that I possibly could. When I lost my family, not only did I grieve their losses but I also lost my coping mechanism, so the symptoms of my child abuse came tumbling off the shelf to complicate all my new grief.

Dr. Denson-Gerber believed that my PTSD might be causing elevated cortisol levels that could be preventing me from getting pregnant. She suggested I see an endocrinologist to diagnose and treat any chemical imbalance I might have and hopefully increase my odds of getting pregnant. Judi understood how important having children was to me, especially in light of my past, and she wanted to help. She validated the measures I was taking to cope with my grief, and she encouraged me to stand firm in my faith and to continue to talk with Dr. Matefy. She too believed that John was my God-appointed grief partner and that in many ways he was the reason I was still alive. I agreed. I left Judi's office that day depressed but with more determination than ever to get back on the road to healing and moving forward.

CHAPTER 9

Touched by Angels

But those who trust in the LORD will find new strength.
They will soar high on wings like eagles. They will run and
not grow weary. They will walk and not faint.

—ISAIAH 40:31 NLT

"He's going to hit you!" Kim Carlyle exclaimed.
Kim's husband, Kyle, swerved as the tractor-trailer
passed his car and careened into the lane in front of him. The
Carlyles were headed north on the Florida Turnpike, traveling
to Disney World with their children. At first, the tractor trailer,
with its passenger casually dangling his foot outside the window,
distanced itself from the Carlyle's vehicle and continued right
until it crossed into the emergency lane and suddenly leapt into
the air, hitting a parked car on the paved shoulder as if it were
taking on a speed bump without slowing down. The tractor
trailer jackknifed, flipped on its side, and skidded to a stop
a quarter mile down the road. The parked car instantly burst
into flames as a white pickup truck in the left lane slammed on
its brakes to avoid crashing into the tractor-trailer, only to be
rear-ended by the blue car driving behind it. A man and woman
jumped out of the pickup truck and ran toward the blazing car.
Another man came running up from the line of traffic stacking
up behind the accident.

In shock, Kim dialed 911 on her husband's car phone as
they observed the horrific scene. She told them that a truck had

hit a car and that the car was on fire in the emergency lane of the turnpike south of the Jupiter exit. Just then, Kim recalled that I emerged from the opening created by the shattered windshield of the burning car. The two men who had run to the burning car began shouting, "Take my hand!" but I was obviously confused. Kim said I began crawling back into the car before one of the men grabbed my hand and pulled me through the shattered windshield. Kim pleaded with the dispatch to hurry, that there was somebody inside the car.

When she hung up, she and her husband instructed their children to stay in the car, and then they ran to help. The flames had grown to twenty feet high, and the smell of gasoline and smoke filled the air as the Carlyles approached the scene. I was badly burned. My hair was smoking, and my body and clothes were charred.

Impulsively, I broke away from my two rescuers and ran back toward the car, screaming, "My life is in that car!" One of the men grabbed me just before I could dive back into the flames, and together they set me down in the grass against the median barrier a good distance from the car.

The Carlyles joined the crowd gathering around me. I was in shock and confused. My brain couldn't process what had just happened. I could not grasp the severity of my injuries, let alone the likelihood that my family was dead. I only continued screaming out to the surrounding crowd to do something to help, because "my life was in that car."

Hearing my desperate pleas upset Kyle, and he returned to his car to check on the kids. Neither he nor his wife wanted them to know what was happening. Kim told me that she had called 911 and that the ambulance was on its way.

Another man ran up and said the driver of the tractor-trailer needed help. The two men who had rescued me hopped to their feet. One of them instructed the crowd to hold onto me so I would not run back to the fireball, and they left to attend to the driver of the tractor trailer. There I sat, alone, surrounded by the crowd, hysterically crying out for anyone to help as the flames blazed and engulfed the car with my family trapped inside.

Just then, a man approached me. He was about six foot three with dishwater blond hair and was wearing a windbreaker. He knelt in front of me, called me by name, and then spoke softly into my ear. I do not remember him and cannot recall what he said. No one else heard his words as he whispered too quietly for anyone around me to hear. But I finally stopped screaming and crying for my family and no longer tried to jump up and run back to the car. I was distraught, but I was told his words calmed me as I listened intently.

After what felt like an eternity to Kim, the paramedics arrived, and as they entered the circle to tend to me, the tall man stood and exited. Impressed and appreciative of how he had comforted me in my desperation, Kim followed the tall man to thank him. As he exited the circle, she lost sight of him for a second, and when she exited the circle after him, he was gone. The man was too large to miss or overlook, but with no vehicle within twenty-five yards of the circle of people, the man had disappeared.

Kim Carlyle did not include the tall stranger in her recollection of that day during her interview after the accident. Instead, she pulled my attorney Chris Searcy aside beforehand to tell him. Mrs. Carlyle appeared shaken up when she talked about the mysterious man who had helped me, but no one could provide her any further details on this man's whereabouts. The man did not fit the description of any of the witnesses attorney Searcy had found and interviewed. What struck him was that the man's description fit John Berger, but that was impossible, since John was at home in Connecticut at the time of the accident. With no explanation outside of the supernatural, Chris proceeded to interview Mrs. Carlyle. Much like her, he decided to wait for the appropriate time to share her testimony with me.

It was three weeks shy of three years since the accident. John and I decided to focus our attention back on getting pregnant. I took Dr. Gerber's advice and made an appointment with the fertility specialist, who provided hope. She said my blood tests showed significantly elevated cortisol levels, and that alone could prevent me from getting pregnant. If we were able to lower those levels and then attempt IVF, my odds of a successful pregnancy would increase. So she recommended I go on medication for one month to balance out my cortisol levels. After that month, I could try another IVF cycle. I cautiously clung to that new hope, but I needed to trust in God's plan rather than set myself up for more heartbreak. I was still locked in the emotional prison of when something good happened, something bad would follow.

When my friend Liz told me that it took her three years to begin to feel better after the drowning death of her child, I circled that day on my calendar. But when it arrived, I realized there was no magic in that day. My healing was on the Lord's schedule, not on a day circled on my calendar.

HEART OF
THE MATTER

The first song of my family's funeral Mass was one which I believe was a love letter from Dawn for me, a reminder to always remember this song. She and I sang it together in choir at our church and we both embraced its message to not live in fear. "When you go through deep waters, I will be with you. When you go through rivers of difficulty, you will not drown. When you walk through the fire of oppression, you will not be burned up; the flames will not consume you" (Isa. 43:2).

He says, "Come to me,
all you who are weary and burdened,
and I will give you rest."

—Matthew 11:28 NIV

I really wanted that rest. I was exhausted—physically, spiritually, and emotionally—and I needed to rest. "Lord," I prayed, "please heal me. Please give me the grace I need to move forward through this desert I am in."

I was tired of being tired and depressed. My hold on Him at times may have felt like it was slipping, but I would come to realize that His hold on me was strong and faithful.

As I trudged through the next month, I had another dream that toyed with my sanity.

In the dream, I was having a conversation with an unfamiliar woman who said, "We feel that you are well enough to have Dawn back."

"What about Stephen and Michael?" I asked.

"Yes, they're fine. You just have the *best* children. They are so good."

The dream continued as I next found myself in my kitchen, talking to John.

"I just can't believe it," I told him. "I convinced her I can have all three of them back."

When I awoke, I was overjoyed and relieved to be getting my children back. The dream felt so real that it took time for me to realize it was just a dream. When I did, it crushed me. It was like my children had died all over again, and I cried inconsolably, waking up John.

Then I sank back into my pillow, defeated. I missed them all so much, and they were slipping further away from me. Three years had passed, and it was getting harder to recall the touch, sight, and smell of those I had loved so well. They were slowly fading from my senses even as I desperately groped the past to keep them with me.

After a month, the medication trial successfully lowered my cortisol levels and we tried another IVF cycle.

It failed.

Despondent over the loss, I sought refuge in a local bookstore. I tore through seemingly every new study or piece of literature that dealt with grief, yet my appetite was insatiable. Reading grief books had comforted me through my anxiety and fear, and I needed a special dose of consolation that day. It could not be from just anyone, either. I needed someone who lived through what I had or someone who had a great deal of empathy and life experiences to mentor me.

As I perused the selections, I found what I sought: a lone, dusty, beat-up copy of a book that, oddly enough, I had never seen despite its familiar author. It was as if God had sent an angel to place that book in my sight that day.

The first time I had the opportunity to read another book of this genre, I had taken a pass. I had been assigned to read Dr. Elisabeth Kübler-Ross's landmark study *On Death and Dying* as a nursing student around the time my grandmother had passed away, but with my anxiety about death smothering me back then, I had skipped that assignment. Eighteen years later, seeking comfort for the losses of Gerry and the kids and staring at a copy of *On Children and Death* on the shelf in front of me, I knew I had to read it. That night, I opened the book as well as the floodgates to my emotions. I read each page through torrents of tears but felt uplifted and more peaceful than I had felt since before Gerry and the children had died.

"Lord, please take care of Gerry, Dawn, Stephen, and Michael and tell them how much I love and miss them. And please help me because I'm not doing very well right now, and I need You to carry me because I'm not sure I can take another step."

I read the entire book that night, and the next day I wrote to Dr. Kübler-Ross. I told her my story and thanked her for her work and for giving me hope in my grief. A warm feeling of peace and calm came over me as I mailed that letter. I didn't know if she would respond, but just putting those thoughts on paper made my heart feel lighter. Two weeks later there was an envelope in my mailbox. Dr. Kübler-Ross had written back to me. Hands trembling, I rushed into the house to read her reply.

October 12, 1992

My Dear Donna,

Thank you for your letter, which I am just reading today. You do have to come to one of my workshops. We are sending you the schedule and the list of their whereabouts. If you can come to one of the workshops that we have in Head Waters, maybe we will have the chance to talk to each other. Except for the November workshop in Head Waters, I plan to attend probably most, if not all, of them.

You need a deeper healing for the loss of your children before you are ready to have more children. That will help you tremendously. You know they are all together, and they are having a ball. They are surrounded with love, humor, joy, and peace. My feeling is that until you can experience all those things again, you should not add to your family. I would be glad to help you. Just call our office at the above number and talk to Linda. She can tell you when we have an opening at the next workshop.

My love and blessings to you,

Elisabeth

"They are all together and they are having a ball."

Somewhere deep within my soul, I felt it to be true, and my empty, broken heart welcomed a touch of joy. I immediately began to make plans to attend one of Elisabeth's workshops.

Meanwhile, I had not abandoned my letter-writing campaign. One of my main interests was in compelling the trucking industry to adopt more stringent safety requirements, and now there was a new piece of legislation that sought to lessen the regulations on the trucking industry. This was not a matter of politics for me; it was, however, one of life and death. I could not trust that this tragedy would not happen to me again or put someone else I loved or another innocent family through the horror that had become my existence.

Through Chris Searcy, I became involved with an organization called Citizens for Reliable and Safe Highways (CRASH) and began my letter-writing campaign. I told individuals, the media, and groups about what had happened and pleaded with lawmakers, public officials, members of the Department of Transportation, and anyone who would listen to not let this legislation pass. I enlisted family, friends, and even classrooms of children to write letters with me. Together with the public relations staff of Chris Searcy's law firm, we also produced a video and cover letter that was sent to close to one hundred members of Congress.

While this piece of legislation allowed me to channel my grief into something productive, it did not distract me from the constant reminders that haunted me. On days when I felt good and thought I had set my grief aside, Gerry and the kids still occupied my thoughts, words, and actions. I was so entangled in grief that I did not even realize how much I was internalizing those feelings every moment of every day. It had been over three years, and I could not help but ask myself "Will I ever feel better?"

These thoughts were met with yet another dream. I was standing on a corner as Dawn stood on the street corner across from me. She was waving to me with a big smile on her face, and I wondered if she was older, because she looked thinner and possibly taller, but I was not sure. Stephen and Michael were with her, and I knew they were all happy.

When I woke up, I had no illusions that I was getting them all back, contrary to the last dream. In the first dream I had of Dawn, she had told me she helped children cross to the other side. In this dream, she was standing on the opposite side of the street from me. The fact that she was across the street had obvious significance. I had last seen my family on a roadway, and that was where they had parted from this earth and continued to heaven while I was left behind. Despite the comfort of that dream, I could not help but miss them so much.

Through my contact with Alive Alone, I learned of the milestone called "reinvesting." Just because I was suddenly childless did not mean I was no longer a parent. I just was not a "practicing parent" anymore, and I needed to take the love and time I shared with Dawn, Stephen, and Michael and reinvest it in ways that would preserve treasured memories, provide healing, and bring me peace.

This was a difficult challenge. John and I still had not given up on our hopes of getting pregnant, but if those efforts did not succeed, Alive Alone members shared options like adoption and foster children or Big Brothers, Big Sisters and other similar volunteer programs. Another possibility would be to come to terms with surrendering the parent role and going in another direction altogether. John and I weren't there yet, but it was comforting to know that Alive Alone would be there to support me if that time came.

We decided to move forward with another IVF attempt. I was not sure I could tolerate another failure. We had been praying for a child for so long without receiving answers that we could not help but feel that God had other plans. Matthew 7:8–9 (NLT) says, "For everyone who asks, receives. Everyone who seeks, finds. And to everyone who knocks, the door will be opened. You parents—if your children ask for a loaf of bread, do you give them a stone?"

I had been asking the Lord for bread for two years, and in my low times, I felt like I was only getting stones in return, but I would not allow my discouragement to compromise my faith. I reminded myself that I had to trust that God would make sense of all this in His time. Deep inside I felt like He was moving mountains for me that I just couldn't see during that time. He was creating the foundation in me for a future that would give Him glory. A future of resilience and strength.

HEART OF
THE MATTER

Resilience doesn't mean that we don't experience grief. And resilience doesn't take away our pain; it enables us to manage it. Resilience sees beyond our pain and allows us to keep our focus on Christ. In the storms of life, we continue to trust in God because we are resilient and know that He is our refuge and our deliverance. We are not swallowed up by adversity because we trust that He is faithful. Resilience gets us through the tough times, those times of darkness and pain, and allows us to continue forward with eternity in our heart.

Consider these words of the resilient prophet Habakkuk:

Even though the fig trees have no blossoms,
and there are no grapes on the vines;
even though the olive crop fails,
and the fields lie empty and barren;
even though the flocks die in the fields,
and the cattle barns are empty,
yet I will rejoice in the Lord!
I will be joyful in the God of my salvation!

—Habakkuk 3:17–18

CHAPTER 10

Two Steps Forward, One Step Back

For truly, I say to you, if you have faith like a grain of mustard
seed, you will say to this mountain, "Move from here to there,"
and it will move, and nothing will be impossible for you.

—MATTHEW 17:20 ESV

It was almost four years since the crash, and I was riding
a wave of optimism toward its crest as the airplane touched
down in Charlottesville, Virginia. A few weeks back I had gained
a large victory when the letter-writing campaign I had joined
with CRASH persuaded the trucking industry to withdraw its
proposal calling for an increase in truck drivers' hourly limits
under the North American Free Trade Agreement. In a few
short months of advocacy, I was able to accomplish more than
I could have dreamed of. Additionally, we were in the middle
of another IVF cycle. Soon I would know if I was pregnant. As
I ventured out to Dr. Elisabeth Kübler-Ross's "Life, Death, and
Transition Workshop," I was so full of hope.

The charming red-brick Charlottesville Airport was beau-
tifully decorated for the holidays. It housed only one conveyor
belt within its baggage area, and with so few people, I breezed
through baggage claim and ventured out into the cold mountain air to await the van to my destination. There, I met Eileen,
a fellow traveler and nurse who agreed to give me my daily
IVF injections, and others who were traveling with us to the
workshop. A nervous excitement filled the air as we chatted

until our transport arrived. Moments later, we all loaded into the fifteen-passenger van and headed south on Route 29 until we reached I-64 West.

Ever since the accident, I had difficulty driving on the highway. I would take the most circuitous path to avoid it, but not having a say in this van's route, I tried to hide my anxiety as we pulled onto the freeway. Within minutes we were amid the steep inclines and sharp drop-offs of the Blue Ridge Mountains. Thankfully, this scenic four-lane highway had little traffic, but as the snow fell and the brakes struggled to engage the icy road on those declines, my terror grew. Head Waters, Virginia, was forty miles away, and every inch that van traveled felt like it would be the last before it went careening off one of the many overlooks. Squeezing my eyes closed and gripping the seat, I kept reminding myself that as treacherous as this road was, there was a greater reward on the other side. If I could just grit my teeth and bear the fear and anxiety of this journey, I would soon be in a calm and peaceful place, a place full of love and healing. I so desperately wanted to make it to my destination.

When the van finally arrived at the ranch, a hexagonal wood structure emerged through the Virginia pines as we drove over the gravelly path and parked. Puffs of my breath preceded me as I exited the van and labored toward the double doors with my suitcase in tow. There was no sign to direct us and no one to greet us, so I chose the closest entrance. Once inside, I was aware of only two things—the blast of warm air that neutralized the icy outdoors and the hospital bed off to one side of the room. The pathos of a life-sized figure of a cancer patient who lay dying in the bed was only eclipsed by the caring pose of the larger-than-life angel sculpture leaning gently over the body with her wings at half-span and arms outstretched. The angel was patiently awaiting that last breath. I stood transfixed as thoughts of an angel like that greeting everyone I had ever loved and lost raced through my head.

The vignette slowly faded away when a voice broke the tranquility of the moment.

"Are you here for the workshop?"

Still collecting myself, all I could manage was "Uh, uh, yes."

"Okay then, let me show you where to put your things," the staff member replied.

I entered yet another hexagonal-shaped room with beds all around. A few women were unpacking their things, and we quickly bonded as more and more women who would be sharing this room arrived. The people represented myriad backgrounds and callings, and our conversations rolled minutes into hours until the time came to meet the benefactor who had gathered all forty of us into her home.

I would never forget the first time I saw Dr. Elisabeth Kübler-Ross. She was chopping vegetables in the center kitchen with a cigarette hanging limply from her lips. I would soon learn that, in addition to her cigarettes, Dr. Kübler-Ross adored fresh, healthy eating and would wake around 4:30 a.m. to pick vegetables out of her garden or greenhouse (depending on the season) and begin cooking for the day. The only way I could reconcile the irony of a health-conscious physician who smoked was that Dr. Kübler-Ross's true concern lay in the health of the spirit more than the body. She was so certain of an afterlife when her time on earth came to an end that she did not worry about death.

In a short amount of time, one thing became apparent about Elisabeth—she was an absolutely amazing woman. She had turned her ranch into a getaway camp for rehabilitation of the mind and spirit. Forty of us were fortunate enough to be welcomed into her home, where we slept in bunk beds as if we were back in college just beginning our lives. I guess in some ways we were.

People alternated shifts helping Elisabeth prepare the food, and we all helped clean up after each meal. There was something magically communal about sharing the entire process of a meal with a group of people. By tending to each other's most basic needs, we developed an expedited trust for each other. This group of men and women that would spend the greater part of the next five days together became a caring and loving community almost immediately.

The first morning of the workshop, we learned that the bond we created the night before at dinner ran far deeper than we had ever imagined. It was striking how many of us already knew each other and our stories. Still, we began by introducing ourselves and sharing the life event(s) that brought us to the workshop. Each story was more painful and poignant than the next. Then Elisabeth began to speak. As she conveyed her impeccable understanding of people and grief, she had us hanging on her every word. She had traveled extensively during her research on death and dying, and this workshop reflected her global outreach, with people attending from all over the country and world.[1]

Elisabeth's knowledge of grief was not limited to those who are bereaved. She helped me to reach the understanding that there is a commonality in grief. Whatever our loss, the characteristics of grief are universal. We respect the details of each other's loss but focus on those characteristics we hold in common. This concept helped explain a lot about several people I had encountered on my grief journey. At the time I did not fully appreciate the grief of a friend whose daughter was facing a potentially debilitating eye disease, when my own daughter had just died. In time, grief created in me a well of understanding and compassion. Loss is not a competition. Whatever type of loss you suffer, we all bear the sorrow of pain and grief in our hearts.

One important point that Elisabeth stressed was how important it was to address *all* our grief. We do not grieve the person, dream, or hope we lost in a vacuum. We grieve every role that the person, dream, or hope held in our life. Conversely, we grieve every role that we no longer hold in that person, dream, or hope. The question becomes "How do we do that?"

Elisabeth was very practical and shared some ideas on how to grieve all that we had lost. She encouraged us to pack a lunch and go to the cemetery (or a similar meaningful place) to rest and talk. We would go through everything we needed to say that we never had the chance to express before our loss. Elisabeth called it "taking care of old business." If we do not resolve the problems stemming from our old business, resolving our grief and moving forward would be much more complicated.

I hung onto Elizabeth's every word. I took notes upon notes, each pearl of wisdom providing great truth and hope.

One very important concept was that of acceptance. Most people are not ready for that in early grief, but it is important as time goes on to face the reality of our loss. It is always easier to take the path of least resistance, but a quick fix to avoid pain is not always the best thing for us in grief. We want to preserve our psychological and emotional health, and that requires us to face the reality of our situation in spite of how painful that may be. It's our decision if we want to follow the path of insubmissive grief and cling to our loss and trials or if we want to move beyond the shadow of our grief and find light and joy again.

HEART OF THE MATTER

Being Christian does not take away our natural response to loss. When Jesus heard His friend Lazarus died, John 11:35 tells us, "Jesus wept." Being human obligates us to the grief journey in times of loss. But every healthy response to loss eventually reaches a point of acceptance. We are not obligated to deem the loss as "good," but nor can we keep looking away, making believe it didn't happen. If we are to experience the abundant life the Lord has for us, we are called to accept the reality of our loss.

I own my grief. I do not try to put it behind me, to get over it. To forget it. And with the grace of God, I am able "to go beyond just merely owning my grief, toward owning it *redemptively.*"

—Nicholas Wolterstorff, from *Lament For A Son*[2]

Elisabeth's advice covered the entire spectrum of how we respond to loss. She then went on to describe a three-stage model of death. The first is the physical stage, the second, a stage of psychic awareness where we may see loved ones who died before us, and the third is a stage of light and knowledge. I could not help but think about John 1:4–5 (NLT), which says, "The Word gave life to everything that was created, and His life brought light to everyone. The light shines in the darkness, and the darkness can never extinguish it."

I pictured Gerry, Dawn, Stephen, and Michael as a part of that light. They had overcome darkness and death and were alive in the truth and light of God. I was happy for them, and even though my heart still ached, I wanted to be a part of their light.

After Elisabeth finished speaking, we broke into smaller groups, each with an assigned group leader. In these sessions, each of us got up and spoke for as long as we needed. We told our stories, expressed our pain, discussed ways to cope, and, more than anything else, we cried. These tears were good tears. They were productive tears. They were tears that were spilled where we were surrounded by the warmth of understanding hearts rather than the solitude of our loneliness. It was hard work and so draining. But with such intensive support, I felt like I was chiseling away large stones, rather than tiny pebbles, from my mountain of grief.

At one point, I broke away from the group and went to the kitchen for a cup of tea, where I found myself alone with Elisabeth. She was preparing food for dinner that evening, and I took the opportunity to introduce myself. Elisabeth immediately remembered me from our correspondence and expressed how happy she was to see me. We chatted a bit, and, at one point, she astounded me with a revelation.

"You know, Donna, God has special plans for you," she said. "Why else do you think He allowed you to be put through the tumbler like He has?"

I was familiar with Elisabeth's analogy. We were like rocks in the tumbler of life that start out with sharp edges, cracks, and flaws, but have the potential to become shiny, smooth gems. As we tumble through the heartaches, losses, and disappointments in life, the pain is excruciating, but we emerge a polished new creation.

So much did not make sense about the crash. How could I reconcile a loving, merciful God with the death of my family? I never once thought God ordained our tragedy, but couldn't He have intervened and prevented it?

When God created humanity, He didn't force us to love Him. He set us in the garden with an open gate and an invitation engraved on our heart to choose Him.

God did not shield His own Son, Jesus, from the consequences of the evil actions of others, and He became a part of Jesus's suffering as the grieving Father. He did so to show the depths of His love for us and His desire for us to choose Him so we would have eternal life.

When I looked at it through this lens, I saw a God who was part of my suffering and who was grieving with me. That's when I made the decision to trust that He would put the pieces of my life back together. Like rocks in a tumbler, the trials of life are opportunities for us to embrace the Lord's faithful presence and allow Him to lovingly smooth the rough edges and seal up the cracks and flaws created by the losses that inevitably assail us.

HEART OF THE MATTER

Loss is an inescapable and painful part of life. We alone make the choice to allow it to chain us in a prison of despair or use it as an opportunity to grow and open our hearts to hope. When we make life-affirming choices, we gain understanding, compassion, gratitude and strength. We grow closer to the Lord and find ourselves becoming the person He wants us to be.

Here on earth you will have many trials and sorrows.
But take heart, because I have overcome the world.

—JOHN 16:33

Sorrow and the opportunity for healing were on full display for those of us attending this workshop. Each story was more powerful than the previous one. Even the lives where God was not acknowledged had His handprints all over them. There were survivors of unimaginable abuse; those who had lost parents, siblings, spouses, and children; and a young man dying of AIDS. I made friends with a young woman whose three-year-old son had died on the Fourth of July when a firework malfunctioned and exploded into the crowd. Her story reminded me of the injustice of mine, and I knew her pain and the desire she had to make a difference for others.

In the safety of the workshop, we felt comfortable sharing our innermost thoughts and feelings without fear of reprisal. At one point, a woman approached me from across the room and blindsided me with something a stranger in a different setting likely would never divulge.

"I just had to come over here," she told me. "I was looking at you from across the room, and I saw you with a baby in your arms."

I tried to stay composed as I told her how hard it was to hear that. I told her about my attempts to get pregnant and she tried to assure me that her vision was a good thing. She said she had a gift. It was not clairvoyance but the power of discernment. I was unfamiliar with her ability at that time, so I was a bit skeptical as she continued, but she told me she believed I would have a baby.

If the conversation had happened anywhere else, I probably would have dismissed it, but at Dr. Kübler-Ross's workshop, things were different. There was a deeper spiritual connection that we all seemed to be tapping into, maybe just from being in such proximity to Elisabeth, who seemed to radiate spirituality.

Whatever it was, I did not totally disregard what this woman said to me, because I so desperately wanted her to be right.

I learned more about grief throughout the rest of the workshop than during my previous three years of living through it, and my soul was so much more edified than at any other time in my life. My reading and understanding was all so academic up to this point. Authors like Catherine Sanders were helpful in describing the different types of grief, such as my category—the "cumulative grief" of multiple family losses, and then providing tools to help get through it. But with Elisabeth and the people at her workshop, I learned to deal with my grief beyond the physical and intellectual means I had been using.

Elisabeth used a graphic for the four quadrants of our being: physical, emotional, intellectual, and spiritual. She urged us to strive to make each quadrant equal to the other.

Our culture places great emphasis on the physical and intellectual, often at the expense of the emotional and spiritual. Limiting our emotional and spiritual growth throughout our lives could rob us of resilience when tragedy strikes.

I realized I personally had fallen victim to this to some degree. Attention to physical recovery from my injuries was unavoidable and all-encompassing. But, in time, I found myself focusing on physical and intellectual means to try to heal my aching emotional self and suffering spirit. But that would never get me to the deep level of healing that I needed.

Of course, Elisabeth had a very practical recipe for emotional and spiritual healing. Since grief has no schedule, it is healthy for us to step back and take a break from time to time. The most important part of healing is balanced living. If we can refuse to walk in the darkness of negativity and embrace the light of gratitude and love, we will develop the positive attitude we need to feed our soul. When we cultivate our spirituality, we will often find the person we are meant to be. I liked those ideas and was ready to follow Elisabeth's advice.

At one group session, Elisabeth told me I did not give myself any credit for all the grief work I had done. She said I needed to recognize the gains I had made and not to be so hard on myself.

That critique surprised me a bit. I had never thought about acknowledging my own achievements. In my upbringing, there was an expectation that a goal would be accomplished and then, without much fanfare, you would move on to the next goal. Maybe that was why I was so hard on myself, and it was another example of how I needed to allow more room for emotional and spiritual growth, maybe at the expense of my intellect from time to time. In short, I needed to be nicer to myself and take spiritual rests.

Perhaps that is what led to Matthew 6:33 (NIV) becoming my favorite Bible verse. "Seek the kingdom of God above all else and live righteously, and He will give you everything you need."

I left Dr. Kübler-Ross's workshop more energized and uplifted than I had been since the accident. I knew that Jesus Christ was sustaining me, answering my prayers for help in my life, and that He would guide me if I would only continue to listen. I never doubted my family was with God in heaven, "surrounded by love" and "having a ball" as Elisabeth had said. We spoke so often about life after death at the workshop that Elisabeth made it feel like Gerry and the kids were within reach, at least spiritually. I believed strongly that no matter what the future held, we would all be together again in eternity.

Elisabeth's workshop was truly life changing for me. It helped me clean out the clutter of fear, doubt, and pain in my heart, making room for the good news of hope, love, and renewal.

After keeping up with the injections while away, the egg retrieval and transfer went well. Considering my age and history, this was very promising. It felt like everything was finally falling into place. I understood my grief journey better than ever before, and with John's continued support and encouragement, I could finally envision the future as a positive place.

Then, John and I got the call that the IVF attempt failed, and everything got mixed up again. I prayed and asked for strength, comfort, and guidance. I tried to take it in stride and put on a good face, but it was difficult. My relationship with God had just recently grown so much that He was more tangible in my life than He had ever been before. I was growing spiritually and turning my life over to the Lord, so maybe that was why receiving this news hurt so badly. I knew God was there, I could feel Him, and He knew how much I wanted this. I felt I received yet another stone instead of the bread I prayed for, yet I was able to turn to Him for comfort.

Through it all, John would often say that he was as "constant as the northern star." Unlike Shakespeare's Julius Caesar, it was not a point of pride for John but a statement of fact. He was my best friend, confidant, and greatest support. He insisted we take a walk together with Battle Dog every day, even if it ended up being late at night, and he also helped me plant and care for my fragrant rose garden. While I had never watched sports, he turned me into a diehard fan of the New York Yankees and college basketball. Watching games together was a favorite pastime. John was the glue God sent to hold me together.

My time with Elisabeth had torn down many of the walls of fear and isolation that had imprisoned me. Further strengthened by John's support, I felt a sudden urge to reach out to all the people I could think of who had helped me. I wanted to thank them and let them know that they offered me a lifeline when I was drowning. So I went back to the beginning, and the first person with whom I could remember speaking about my losses and my grief was Michael, the psychologist at Shands Hospital. I could not have gotten through those first days without him, and I wrote him the following letter:

Dear Michael,

Over and over, I think of you and my month at Shands. Recalling my hospitalization makes me very anxious and depressed, so I really try not to focus on it. Yet remembering you and Linda and Charlie and others leaves me with an unsettled feeling—a wish to be able to talk with you all once again. It's like I have some unfinished business with you all, but I'm not sure what. I know that you, Michael, stand out foremost in my mind always.

Although I can only recall dribs and drabs of our conversations, my "sense" of you is that you were my lifeline; you gave me the seeds of courage to accept what had happened and the hope to continue on. I can recall your face vividly when you told me that I would go on to add a "new branch onto the tree of life." That phrase has been with me as has a comforting sense that thoughts of you impart through my many hours of tears. Somehow, I am sure my subconscious recalls all our conversations while the conscious is only able to recall the feelings and emotions surrounding them. I often remember what a wonderful and caring person you are, and I am so grateful to have been brought to Shands and to have you care for me.

Sincerely,

Donna Berger

I wrote a number of letters to people who had been so good to me and considered it a blessing to have still more on my list. The exercise became an inventory of the many people from all walks of life whom God had used to ensure the survival of His injured little lamb.

It felt like my healing was experiencing a growth spurt, and my energy seemed to multiply itself. When the call came out that English language tutors were needed to teach literacy classes to single mothers at the Mercy Learning Center, I could feel the Holy Spirit within convicting me, so I signed up and began my training. Thinking back to Elisabeth's workshop that had changed my life so dramatically, I knew I was supposed to take care of old business first, but I preferred to avoid my past for the time being. I didn't want anything to interrupt this new wave of enthusiasm. So I skipped straight to the step in which I would form my new identity with novel relationships and roles for the future.

Just a few days later, CBS's *Street Stories* segment on trucking industry service hours aired with my interview. A national audience was finally made aware of all the dangers that lax regulations posed for families like mine every day. With the grace of the Lord and those individuals He placed in my life to support me, I was making a difference.

During my first visit with Dr. Matefy after I returned from Elisabeth's workshop, I was able to speak about my grief more objectively. I told him that my sense of loss did not fade, but knowing that the children were okay—no longer with me, but okay—made it tolerable. As Elisabeth would have said, they lived their life here, did what they had to, and moved on. None of that changed my reality or eliminated the agonizing grief of losing them. That would necessitate moving mountains. Very large mountains. But I felt I was gaining ground.

"Time does not feel like it is healing," I told Bob. "It gives you the ability to distance yourself, but when you let yourself remember, the pain is still excruciating. You can put the memories aside more easily, but when you don't, it's just as overwhelming. And then sometimes you can't put them aside. That shadow grief eventually catches up with you."

Little did I know how soon that would happen. At night, I started having this sense I was going to scream, like it was just going to come out of me as I was lying there in bed. Then I began to wonder if this feeling was a sort of visceral memory of when I was screaming immediately after the crash. There had to be a part of me that remembered something, because when I felt this type of depression, it was as if I knew something could not identify its origin. Since Elisabeth's workshop, I could reason and make sense of most of my grief, but not this. I had this feeling that there was something at play that I could not quite grasp from my unconscious. There was this unexplainable sadness. Whatever I had just done, seen, or heard reflected something on the outer limits of my memory.

Perhaps, part of my anxiety could be attributed to a dream I had of Michael screaming. Could that be it? I remembered seeing Michael with his hands in front of his face and his mouth open, shielding himself from the heat and flames. Judianne thought I probably did see him screaming and that I unearthed that quick flash of memory, while the rest of what happened remained buried in my subconscious. I remembered his face; that devastating image would not go away.

I was falling into one of the deep troughs of my grief journey. More and more, I felt the strain of the years. If experts asserted that losing a spouse carried a grief period of three to five years and each child could take ten years to a lifetime to complete the process, how long would it be for a husband and three precious children? I shuddered to think it could be never.

Then the proposal to extend the hours of service for truckers reemerged in the North American Free Trade Agreement, which required redoubling my efforts if I wanted to try and prevent that. Meanwhile, my biological clock continued to count down. We had not tried another IVF attempt since the failed January attempt. Amidst that dark cloud, a most providential light shined through.

As we took off on a flight to Florida, I opened a *Cosmopolitan* magazine that had been left in the seat pocket in front of me. Skimming through its pages, my eyes glossed over meaningless articles and mindless entertainment until they locked onto one tiny blurb tucked into the corner of a page.

The article was about Dr. Richard J. Paulson of the University of Southern California's In Vitro Fertilization Clinic (now known as USC Fertility). Dr. Paulson was relating the latest news on IVF for older women who had a previous pregnancy and were experiencing infertility. I got chills as I read this encouraging message. The woman being described in the article was me! I had reached the end of the road with infertility, and this seemed to be my one last glimmer of hope. I have to admit in my excitement I did something uncharacteristic for me: I tore the page out of the magazine so I could contact the doctor in California when I got home. But before I could move forward through what felt was likely the only door left, I knew I had all kinds of old business to take care of, and, at last, I was ready.

CHAPTER 11

Acceptance and Surrender

This is the day that the LORD has made;
let us rejoice and be glad in it.

—Psalm 188:24 ESV

W hat do you ask for when what you loved most in the world is gone? How do you respond when facing unimaginable change? Answers to these questions did not come immediately, and maybe they were not meant to. Perhaps the answers were supposed to be revealed over time.

I had embarked on a journey to learn how to live again. But the path unfolding before me was littered with roadblocks and detours. The litigation, in many ways, had been a driving force that had kept me going. It was there to focus my mind and energy, and it could occupy all my time when I let it. There was always the next thing—the next deposition, the next mediation, the next trial date—but as much as I had become attached to the emotional ebbs and flows of the case, I realized it was a major roadblock for me. Dr. Offerdahl told me that I would not be able to become pregnant until I lowered my stress and got my cortisol levels under control, and Dr. Kübler-Ross wrote me suggesting that I should not, from an emotional standpoint, have any more children until I moved further along the grief process. Medical and psychological experts were telling me that I had to come to terms with my loss to even have a chance at having the family I so desperately wanted. And at thirty-nine years of age, my time was running out.

I needed to reach the elusive final stage of my grief process: acceptance for what had happened. This was essential for the reorganization of my life and the investment of emotional energy into the future. But it was so difficult to know how to achieve that. I was trying hard to lean on my faith and act out of my trust in God, so I chose to believe He had a hand in leading Dr. Matefy to approach the topic of acceptance with me.

Acceptance was necessary to provide my heart with the serenity and peace it needed to take that first real step into "tomorrow." Acceptance is not giving in and giving tragedy a hall pass. It's not forgetting or even forgiving, which is a very separate process. Acceptance is leaving denial behind and staying within the framework of reality. This takes strength and courage, which are qualities I still pray for daily. I found that acceptance is also a process that we must commit to daily, as it is very easy to feel crushed under the weight of it.

I realized I had developed a more tolerant attitude over the past couple years, but I still was far from complete acceptance of my situation. I never considered that I could not be delivered from my sorrow and pain on this earth, yet I was still suffering. What happened to me was terrible, it was my reality, and if I hoped to heal and move forward in my life, I had to accept it. The emotional "me" would cry when seeing Halloween candy or when hearing the laughter of children, and that was okay as long as it was the inner guided wiser self who made the decisions for my future. Acceptance was not a "woe is me" attitude of giving up. It wasn't about saying "Gerry and the kids and gone that's okay, I'm over it." Because it's *not* okay, and I will *never* be over it. It was also not a head down, shoulder drooping acceptance that would lead to a reclusive, meaningless existence. I needed an acceptance that led me to stand tall and confident in the Lord. But how does a sad, lonely, worn-out traveler on a grief journey find true acceptance?

Hope is the first element that is essential for true acceptance. But what is hope?

For me, hope manifested in those undefinable whispers in my heart that seemed to calm me and give me rest. Hope was my mustard seed of faith in God, which miraculously was anchored somewhere beyond the reaches of my pain and grief.

Once we recognize the hope that perches in our heart, we realize that life has a story beyond our sorrow. That will lead us to the next step in true acceptance. We must make a commitment to healing. Committing to healing meant that I had to embrace that fact that my loved ones would never be erased from my heart or memory. When I felt confident that there was an indelible mark on my heart that would keep them alive for as long as I lived, I knew I was ready to take care of old business and say goodbye. In saying goodbye, I understood that there would still be empty spaces and places, but there would also be a life of unknown and even unlimited potential. The Lord had big plans for me, as Elisabeth had said, and it was time for me to find my new place in the world and what those plans entailed.

The first step was to call Chris Searcy and ask him to settle our case. It was a decision a long time in the making.

I had hoped for a "normal" trial, in which everyone told the truth and a jury verdict would be reached in a matter of days or weeks. Instead, I had a truck driver who lied in his deposition, saying that I was driving the car and had cut him off, when all the forensic evidence clearly showed that Gerry was behind the wheel and our vehicle was parked on the side of the road. I myself was subjected to repeated depositions and interviews which had taken their toll, forcing me to relive the nightmare of the crash over and over again.

After nearly three years, two trial delays, two mistrials, and the disqualification of a somewhat hostile judge, I was physically and emotionally drained. It was time. No amount of money could ever replace the loss of my precious husband and children, but settling the case would bring at least a modicum of peace and would perhaps help someone else from ever having to walk in my shoes.

With John speaking on my behalf and Chris and his team's tenacity, an agreement was eventually reached. Still, when the call came in that the case was finally over, I felt like the rug had been pulled out from under me. As soon as Chris finished giving me the news of the settlement, I passed the phone over to John, and I cried and cried and cried. Some were tears of relief, some were from the undeniable realization that my family was never coming back, but mostly it was a funeral, the closure I had never had.

HEART OF THE MATTER

I was beginning to understand that I would grieve forever. But I wasn't frightened by it anymore. I was able to slowly and with great love capture the memories that flooded my mind and place them in keepsake boxes in a special corner of my heart. I knew I would never be the same, nor could I be, but I hoped I would become the person God wanted me to be. It was time for me to fully put my trust and my faith in God. He was still writing the story of my life, and I was ready to listen to the call to surrender to His will for my future. I was ready to be whole again and put a new branch on the tree of life.

I can do all things through Him who strengthens me.
—Philippians 4:13

I went back to my work with CRASH, spearheading another letter-writing campaign in Oregon. It was nice to still have an outlet to use the senselessness of my tragedy to affect some good in the world around me. John and I were blessed in our marriage, and we were dedicated to each other. We had an ever-growing circle of friends, and we enjoyed our coffee runs in the mornings, our volunteer work, cooking together, and our evening walks. I was feeling much lighter, and the support from those closest to us made it feel it was the new beginning we were hoping and praying for.

Time went on and our attempts at having a child simply were not working. It seemed senseless to continue this pattern of heartbreak. The only thing that kept us from giving up entirely was that one little article I had found in the *Cosmopolitan* magazine. That doctor in California had more success with IVF, particularly with older women, than seemingly anyone else, and we felt that if he could not help us, it was unlikely that anyone could. So I made the call. I didn't expect him to call me back so quickly and then spend forty-five minutes talking with me. I sat cross-legged on the bed and told him the whole story from sweet dreams to tragedy and beyond. He was moved by my story and said he truly hoped we would consider a trip to California because he would be honored to have the opportunity to try to help us. John was all in for the trip; he loved the Golden State, and I began to get excited about the prospect as well.

As we began to plan our trip, I sensed a hint of hesitance in John.

"Are you sure this is what you want to do?" he asked one evening.

Still dealing with the symptoms of my PTSD, particularly the habit of second-guessing myself, I began with a litany of "whys, what's the matters, and don't you want to gos?"

It was not that John did not want to go, but this IVF signaled the end of the road. We had to face the fact that if Dr. Paulsen was unable to help us, there would be nowhere else to turn. John worried that if we were not successful, the hope of having children together would be over, and those dreams would be shattered thousands of miles away from any family or friends to support us. It was frightening.

First Corinthians 13:13 (NLT) states, "Three things will last forever—faith, hope, and love . . ." I had fought the good fight of faith, but now John and I stared down the real possibility of losing hope. But we pressed forward anyway, maybe because of the next line of that verse: ". . . and the greatest of these is love."

I called and made the appointment.

There were so many preparations to make in traveling somewhere for an extended period. We had no idea how long we would be in California, but we knew it could be up to several months.

The week before we left, there was one final task I had to accomplish. It was about time I heeded the wisdom of Elisabeth Kübler-Ross and took care of some old business.

Elisabeth had told me I had to first deal with my past before I could plan a future with children, and I realized that this was about a lot more than whether I would be able to get pregnant. It was about my ability to handle the role of mother again. To move past my grief and toward acceptance, I would have to let go of the idea that I was in control of anything, and I would have to let go of my loved ones, trusting that they were safely in the loving arms of the Lord.

I drove out to the cemetery to visit my grandmother. It was a beautiful, bright, sunny summer day. I sat down on the ground at her gravesite and mindlessly picked at the blades of grass as I told her I forgave her for those difficult years of my childhood. I told her it took time to reconcile the physical and emotional abuse and that I was sorry I still harbored some feelings of unforgiveness in my heart. I knew she truly loved me, and I told her I thought she did the best she could in her situation.

Accepting my grandmother for who she was didn't mean her behavior was justifiable, but I had to try to understand from her point of view why she would have treated me so roughly. After a long conversation, I told my grandmother that I forgave her for everything, and I thanked her for the many good things she had done for me. Then I let go of all those pent-up emotions, and I embraced the peace that filled my heart.

The next day, I visited my father's grave. I did not have the issues with my dad as I had with my grandmother. He was a great guy, and I loved every minute I got to spend with him.

I told him how difficult it was for me when he passed; I had been so young and unprepared. I wished we could have had more time together, especially early on, and I wished he could have seen his grandchildren. I told him a bit about each of them. He would have been so proud of them, but he was with them now and knew that firsthand.

Finally, I picked a day in which I gathered enough strength to go to Gate of Heaven Cemetery in Trumbull, Connecticut, to visit Gerry, Dawn, Stephen, and Michael. I brought lunch because there was so much on my heart that I needed to say, and that would take time. Thankfully, it was a warm, sunny day.

I told Gerry how sad I was and how much I missed him. I explained that I was worried he felt I was not being true to him by remarrying and trying to have more children. I knew of people who never got remarried and never had more children. Did he think I was betraying him? Did they *all*? That was the last thing I wanted to do. I told him how much I still loved him and the children.

Then I spoke to the children individually. As the tears streamed down my face, I told them how sorry I was that I had not been able to save them from such horrible deaths. More than anything, I hoped that they had not been afraid and did not have terrible pain.

I told Dawn how much I missed her smile and her humor. I missed holding her hand when we went shopping in the mall, making Christmas cookies together, and the touch of her silky hair gliding through my fingers as I braided it.

I told Stephen I missed his bear hugs and kisses. I missed toasting marshmallows in the yard with him and his friends, and most of all, I missed "my buddy" who was always willing to help me with chores around the house.

I told Michael I missed him cuddling in my lap as we read stories, and I missed working on his puzzles with him. I missed the wonder in his eyes when he would discover something new and how he was always getting into some sort of mischief, like the time he almost started a fire by putting his "Ghostbuster guys" in the microwave.

I told them all my heart was broken, and I knew the pain of losing them would never, ever go away. I wouldn't have it any other way because each one of them was a precious gift to me. Death could never take away our love for each other or the priceless moments in time that we had shared. I told them that my sadness was not a lack of faith. It was the heartbreak I felt for the lifetime together that we had lost. Yet, at the same time, I was filled with peace and joy in knowing they were happy in heaven.

As I sat there and thought of each one of them, I somehow knew they would want me to be happy to and to live life to its fullest, just as we had done before the crash. In my mind, I tried to turn the circumstances around. If I had died, I would want them to continue on and embrace all that life had to offer. I would not want them to be consumed by grief or to give up on living. A new branch on the tree of life did not replace one that was already there; it added to the fullness of the tree.

A new family would never replace Gerry, Dawn, Stephen, and Michael, but if it were in God's plan for John and me, it would give meaning and purpose to my life while also honoring theirs. I wanted to make them proud of me and show them that the blessings of the love and joy each one of them gave me were the building blocks of my future. Our family was everything that was good and honorable and right, and without it, I would not have the sense of direction I needed to start over.

Before I left the cemetery, I turned to God. I knew that even when I could not "see" Him, because I was blinded by my tears, He stood nearby, patiently waiting for me to take His outstretched hand. During that pause, He had used people, circumstances around me, and the voice of the Spirit to whisper guidance and direction into my heart.

God is not a God of death. He did not cause the death of my family, but He "causes everything to work together for the good of those who love God and are called according to

His purpose for them" (Rom. 8:28). I believed that while this tragedy of my life did not and likely would never make sense this side of eternity, and, I trusted God would be faithful and use my loss for good according to His purpose.

I would always miss Gerry, Dawn, Stephen, and Michael and feel the pain and longing for the part of my heart they carried away with them. But, on a spiritual level, I had to rejoice for them in their new lives, dwelling in the love of the Lord. And now I had to dedicate myself to surrender and acceptance so I could release them and no longer be mired in the quicksand of tragedy and grief. I needed to see that I still had a future and that I could look forward again. And I desperately hoped it would include the elusive role of "mom" in my life.

In that moment, I realized that for far too long, I had been missing the bigger picture. I had been praying not for His will to be done but for *mine*. John and I had reached the end of the road with fertility treatments, and my mind told me that now was the time to give up, but my heart whispered *Not just yet*.

"I'm trying to hear You, Lord," I prayed. "I'm listening to You. I promise if this one last attempt doesn't work, then I will accept that this is not the path You have laid out for me, but that You have some other plan. I want to be a mom again, yet 'not my will, but Yours be done'" (Luke 22:42 ESV).

I had made my peace. I released my life, worries, and cares to God and trusted He would lift me up and sustain me through it all, just as He had through the past four years. And that included the grief of never having children again. I didn't know what the future held for me, but He did, and I knew He would always be there for me, even if my wish to be a mom again was never fulfilled.

I left the cemetery after a long day, feeling drained but unburdened. I had released my loved ones into the hands of the Lord, and I could move confidently into this uncharted new world with hope in these verses.

Those who plant in tears will harvest with shouts of joy. They weep as they go to plant their seed, but they sing as they return with the harvest (Ps. 126:5–6 NLT).

Feeling liberated from the fear and uncertainty that had been cluttering my heart and set free by genuine acceptance and surrender, I was finally calm. I knew the Lord was making this journey with us. We forwarded our mail, shuttered the house, and said our goodbyes.

Our plane touched down at LAX, and a new journey began. John and I found a tiny one-bedroom apartment on the water, not too far from the IVF Clinic. The building was on stilts, which we thought would be romantic. After the three sleepless nights it took to adjust to the sound of the waves lapping below us, we found it hypnotic.

Unlike previous experiences, the doctors and staff at USC embodied the spirit of California in their warm, friendly, laid-back approach. Dr. Paulsen was genuinely touched by our story, and he voiced how badly he wanted to make this work for us. And with that, the process began.

Outside of the clinic, we were like fish out of water. We were in an unfamiliar location for an indefinite period of time, where we knew no one, and we had no plans to stay there long term. There was no Wi-Fi, no navigation system, and no cell phones to help us acclimate to our unfamiliar surroundings. We spent our days looking up coffee shops, grocery stores, and the like in the "yellow pages." Then we'd drive around town with a printed street map to locate them. We took long walks on the beach and explored the inlets and tide pools created by the Pacific Ocean on the unique stretch of coastline where we were staying. We rested, read, and prepared meals together. We also watched the sunset and the people around us living their lives, all the while recognizing that we were working on our own reentry strategy to join them.

Time passed quickly with us always having something new to see and learn about our host state. As the critical point of the cycle approached, John and I prepared ourselves for the pivotal coming days. The egg retrieval went well, and over the next forty-eight hours, I rested and prayed over the past, the present, and God's will for the future.

The day of the embryo transfer arrived, and we were ushered into a different area of the clinic. Dr. Paulsen was not there that day, but his associate, Dr. Mark Sauer, greeted us. He asked if we would like to see the embryos, and with our unequivocal response, he flipped on the monitor in the corner of the room. I lay there in awe of the cell clusters that formed perfect little flowers: a bouquet of life and promise. There was an immediate and personal bond of deep love joining us to these living flowers. They were not just any flowers, they were a bouquet chosen from the garden of our life together, and the urge to love, cherish, and protect them ran deep. I could not speak, choked by the silent tears of so many emotions.

As the time passed, John and Dr. Sauer engaged in lively conversation about the finer points of surfing, even though John's only experience was watching the Pepperdine surf classes from the beach. Meanwhile, with my eyes closed, I prayed God's blessings on our little flowers and on our future, whatever it may hold.

Finally, I heard John say, "I'll stop talking so you can concentrate, Doc."

"Oh, I finished a long time ago," Dr. Sauer replied. "You're all set, Donna. The nurse will be here in a minute to take you to the recovery room. I really enjoyed our conversation, John, and I wish you both all the best."

In the recovery room, my bed was put in a steep Trendelenburg position, which is a medical term for tipping the head of the bed down about twenty-five or thirty degrees. I had to stay like that for two hours, during which time John kept me laughing with his observations of the unique medical environment around us. I think we were both trying to delay acknowledging the obvious fact that the countdown to our future had begun.

The next few days were critical. With all our medical advances, no one had ever figured out how to make an embryo implant itself into the uterine wall. The miracle of implantation after conception was left to God, and its window of opportunity could sometimes be elusive. There were so many variables that had to align perfectly, but I believed when God willed it, that foundation of life nestled into place. I did not know if that would happen for me, but I trusted if it did not, God had another perfect gift in mind.

John and I decided to relax and just enjoy the next five days before we would learn the results. With no more early morning visits to the clinic, we got up later, sat with our coffee, and watched the surfing classes and triathletes who crossed the beach outside our window. We took in the antiquities at the Getty Museum and went up and down the Santa Monica Pier. We even made a trip to Universal Studios, taking care to avoid any rides that might be too stressful for me.

When the five days had passed, we left for our early morning pregnancy test at the clinic. We rode in silence, with John squeezing my hand the entire ride. Our thoughts and emotions swirled around the atmosphere eliminating our need for words. To be unsuccessful on our last attempt would not only be hope unfulfilled but it would also be the very painful loss of our child or children and our future together. Still, we trusted in God's plan for us.

At the clinic, the blood draw was routine and uneventful, and our nurse promised to call at 2:30 p.m. with the results. Not wanting to sit around the apartment for the rest of the day anxiously awaiting the call, we drove to Beverly Hills and spent the morning walking up and down Rodeo Drive, taking in the storefronts and street side cafés just to make the time go by. We had lunch with every second dragging like the beads of condensation that clung to my glass of iced tea before sliding away. Finally, John and I headed back to our apartment to await the call.

At 2:15 p.m., the phone rang, and John answered.

"I think both of you should get on the phone," the nurse told John, so I picked up the extension in the bedroom and eagerly listened in. "Donna, are you sitting down?"

I sat down on the edge of the bed, my heart racing.

"Yes," I said.

"Congratulations, you are pregnant, and there may be more than one. We will need you back in a week to repeat your blood work."

I barely squeaked out, "Thank you, yes, I'll call back and make the appointment."

I could not believe my ears. After all the heartache and years of pain, torment, and failure, hearing those words sank me to my knees. With my head bowed on my clasped hands, I cried, "Thank you! Thank you! Thank you!" And then I prayed, "Lord, I promise I will do my very best to be deserving of this precious gift."

There was a very pregnant pause as John came into the room. We exchanged glances of shock and maybe even a little disbelief. And then, we clung to each other, our kisses salty from tears of happiness. We were expecting!

All I could think was that this had to be a part of God's plan. I had placed my trust in Him, and He had blessed me. I took Dr. Kübler-Ross's advice to cope with my old business, and I had been ready to move in a different direction if this IVF attempt did not work.

For so long I had been asking, and I clung to 1 John 5:14: "And we are confident that He hears us whenever we ask for anything that pleases Him." But it was not until I truly surrendered to His will that I received such a precious gift.

It was so difficult to not immediately share this joyful news with people like my sister, Nanci, and cousin, Madeline, but it had been suggested that we wait for the follow-up blood work. I knew that in a few short days we would be able to celebrate with everyone, even if it was long distance. When my hCG levels, which measured the "pregnancy hormone," continued to soar in follow-up labs, we were finally able to share the good news with everyone back home, and the amount of rejoicing was beyond measure. But it would remain long distance for a while because John and I needed to spend a few more weeks in California to have our first ultrasound at the clinic and be sure everything was okay before we returned.

Follow-up blood work indicated that we were pregnant with multiples. Having already had four children between the two of us, I was confident that we would be able to manage with God's grace, whatever the outcome. The day finally came for the ultrasound, and it confirmed we were pregnant with twins. There are no words for the joy that filled our hearts that day. John and I held hands with happy tears rolling down our faces as we saw our babies on the screen. We were jubilant, and the staff at the clinic celebrated with us. Our new branch on the tree of life had begun to bloom.

We had not traveled far from the rental during the IVF cycle, but that was all behind us, so we took a trip up the coast to see the breathtaking views of the beautiful city of Santa Barbara. John and I had noticed it was a bit windy before we left, but we paid no attention to it.

As we drove home after a relaxing day, the eastern sky had darkened with what we though was an incoming thunderstorm. When we arrived back at the apartment, I gathered together the paper wrappings from our lunch. But when I opened the car door, the blast of warm air that hit me literally grabbed the trash out of my hand and tossed it in every direction. It was a startling first encounter with the natural phenomenon called the Santa Ana winds and the major wildfires they fueled throughout Southern California. But, having no experience with such a disaster at that time, we did not recognize the potentially catastrophic danger around us. We continued to go about our business as if everything was normal.

Over the next few days, the darkening of the Southern California skyline did not escape our notice, but we were still celebrating the news of the twins that our ultrasound had confirmed. We only caught snippets of the conversations swirling around us about the potential danger headed our way and did not even consider canceling the dinner celebration John had planned that weekend at a storied restaurant in LA.

As we headed out that evening for downtown Los Angeles, the air was so thick with ash that we had to stop at a grocery store to buy a roll of paper towels and some Windex®. Every few minutes John would reach out, spray the windshield, and wipe it with a paper towel so he could see through the smeared mess. It was like driving through a blizzard in New England, and we were so late because of it that John had to explain the circumstances to the hostess for us to even get the table he had reserved days before.

The next morning, smoke and ash blacked out the sunrise, and we finally realized the seriousness of the situation. The Southern California wildfires of 1993 were raging all around us as helicopters and airplanes flew back and forth carrying water to support the brave firefighters battling the blazes on the ground.

The following day we stayed in watching the television coverage of the ongoing crisis. My anxiety began to build. That night, around 2 a.m., we were awakened by a loud commotion of people shouting and sirens wailing. Nearby on the beach, a homeless person had built a campfire. The residents of the area had called the police and were fighting with the man to put out the fire.

As they screamed, "Are you crazy?" they doused his fire with buckets of water. With my heart pounding, I turned to John and said, "John, I'm afraid. I want to go home."

"Okay," he said. "Let's figure it out tomorrow."

John tried to conceal his own concern from me during the rest of that sleepless night, but by noon the next day, things had gotten much worse. Across the street, we watched firefighters struggling to contain the flames dotting the Pepperdine University campus lawn.

"John, we have to leave now," I pleaded.

With that, he booked a flight home, and we began to pack.

As our plane took off from LAX, I breathed a sigh of relief. Holding John's hand, I prayed for God's protection over the firefighters and emergency personnel, the people of Southern California, and the dangerous situation we left behind. Then my attention returned to the twins I was carrying, and I smiled and gave thanks for the promise of what was ahead.

CHAPTER 12

A New Branch on the Tree of Life

To all who mourn . . .
God will give a crown of beauty for ashes,
a joyous blessing instead of mourning,
festive praise instead of despair.
In their righteousness, they will be like great oaks
that the LORD has planted for his own glory.

—ISAIAH 61:3

I was glad to be back in Connecticut, but Malibu would
always be a special place for John and me, despite the
circumstances of our hasty departure. I continued to follow
the situation in what had been our home away from home
and to pray for everyone affected by this natural disaster.
The Southern California wildfires of 1993 consumed three
hundred square miles and destroyed over eight hundred
homes. Fifteen thousand brave firefighters battled the blazes
with sixty-seven of them being injured. In Malibu, where John
and I had stayed, the Santa Anas reached fifty miles per hour,
which whipped the west flank of the fire all the way to the
Pacific Ocean. Across the street, the Pepperdine University
campus was saved only by the skill of the firefighters and the
availability of the nearby water.

In our first days home, family and friends greeted us with
a host of celebrations, but after about ten days, that all came to

a halt when the nausea of pregnancy hit me, earlier and harder than I had ever experienced. As I sat at the kitchen table each morning holding my head in my hands and sipping herbal tea, I reminded myself that midway through the fourth month, just as suddenly as the nausea had come, it would disappear, and I would feel great.

In the interim, I spent much of that time reorganizing my life in my head and reflecting on my journey. As Elisabeth had told me, I had been through the tumbler, and I was ready for the brilliance of the gem. In retrospect, I needed that rock bottom in which I momentarily lost faith in order to gain the belief, hope, and strength necessary to be still and listen to the gentle but steadfast voice of the Spirit that guided me along the way. I had been given a second chance. My "old life" and "new life" merged, no longer separate and distinct but rather memories of yesterday woven into the fabric of tomorrow. I knew that I would never get over what had happened, but I felt like I did not have to hold on so tightly. I would never lose them; they were an indelible part of who I had become. My family would always be a part of my life here on earth, but one day the life we once shared would be restored to its fullness in heaven. I was confident in that.

John and I were so excited about the babies that we got an early start on shopping for cradles, cribs, changing tables, car seats, and even a double stroller. We had recently reconnected with Ted Marino, a friend who had worked with my mom when she was a seamstress. He and his wife had also been pregnant with twins through IVF but had lost their boys midway through the pregnancy. My heart broke for them, knowing both the despair of losing children and the struggle of infertility.

I felt connected by our shared grief, and, after hearing this story, I could have seen myself become fearful for my own pregnancy, but something within me had changed. I was persevering through my battle with grief and I was growing in faith. I spent less time and energy on worry, choosing to place my trust in God instead. For the first time since the accident, I reached a point where my empathy did not threaten my own joy, and both the Marinos and I took comfort in our belief in God's faithfulness in all our lives.

I was inspired by this couple's enthusiasm. Despite their own loss, they welcomed the opportunity to decorate our twins' room. Since the babies would be sharing a nursery, the search was on for a theme that would be suitable for either sex. They presented us with a dizzying array of fabrics before we finally agreed on a happy print based on the book, *A Child's Garden of Verses* by Robert Louis Stevenson. Growing up with this book, I always loved its poems, but reading it as an adult, there was one poem I did not remember that told me I had made the right choice.

To My Mother
Robert Louis Stevenson

You too my mother, read my rhymes
For love of unforgotten times,
And you may chance to hear once more
The little feet along the floor.

The thought that a book of poetry could be a window in time, displaying happy memories of the past as well as promises of the future, made me smile. When we found out we were having a boy and a girl, it only added to the interest of the room. On one side the bedding was trimmed in blue stripes, while the other was in pink. The walls were painted in a soft yellow taken from the print, and the theme was complete with a shiny new copy of *A Child's Garden of Verses* perched on the rocking chair. I could not wait to share its special poems with the children, who had already stolen my heart.

By the time the fourth month rolled in, I was more than ready to give up the nausea and feel healthy again. There was so much to do. John and I had all the fun and excitement of preparing for two new babies but also the more difficult task of organizing and then finalizing the care for my mother and his father. We had to find someone to live in and care for my mother full time. John's father required care as well, and it was up to John to organize that and finish closing out his father's business.

My pregnancy was going well, and the babies were growing and healthy. I could feel myself getting stronger emotionally, although birthdays and anniversaries continued to be met with tears. During those times, I would feel sad and lonely, but I was always blessed by those who remembered with me and lifted me up, each in their own special way.

Four and a half years had passed since that fateful day on the Florida Turnpike, and my work with CRASH helped to produce a large victory for the safety of our country's highways. The North American Free Trade Agreement passed without the provision to increase the hourly limits of truck drivers. I was not sure how much of a difference my effort had made, but what mattered was that blocking this legislation might spare another mother from experiencing my anguish. I continued my work with CRASH in this regard, and John joined in, too, making trips to lobby lawmakers in DC on my behalf when I was too pregnant to travel.

It had been eight years since I had an infant in my arms, so I was also reading up on all the latest developments in childcare as well as going through a book of names. We were trying to prepare as best we could, because we knew that once the babies arrived, our focus would be completely on them, and, for a while at least, there would be little time for anything else.

Throughout this new season in my life, it was amazing how much confidence I gained in my ability to move forward. It was as if Isaiah 42:16 (ESV) had been written about me: "And I will lead the blind in a way that they do not know, in paths that they have not known I will guide them. I will turn the darkness before them into light, the rough places into level ground. These are the things I do, and I do not forsake them."

After the crash, I was blind and on an unfamiliar path, but I learned that when I was broken and desperate, God waited patiently at the door of my heart for me to call Him in. And when I did, He lovingly filled me with His Spirit that led me toward surrender and forgiveness.

At first, I had been outraged and angry. I had wanted answers. I had wanted an apology. I had wanted the driver to admit it was his fault that Gerry and the children were dead, but hatred and unforgiveness do not belong in a heart where the Spirit dwells. We forgive because He forgave us. I had to choose to walk in God's ways and forgive unconditionally, without the expectation of apology or payback, trusting that the Lord would be the fair and just judge in His time. When I did, the Lord turned my darkness into light. I felt I had just emerged from that tunnel of darkness, and the sunlight on my face was heavenly. I wanted to shout about it from the rooftop, but my path had been through writing letters, so I continued to reach out to others in that way.

A month before my due date, John and I received a call from our contact at CRASH. Diane Sawyer of *Primetime Live* was interested in filming a segment about our story, so we spoke with the producers about what it would entail and ultimately decided to go forward with the project. John and I would be interviewed, and I would have to gather photos and video of Gerry, the children, and me, starting before the accident and updating my life all the way to the present. They also wanted to film the birth of the babies and their baptism.

It sounded like that could be overwhelming, but the broadcast journalist, Sylvia Chase, and Lee Kamlet, the producer, earned our trust and promised to guide us through it. Ultimately, it would be a way to send out a message of faith and hope to possibly millions of people. If my story could lift up just one viewer who was having a difficult time, it would be worthwhile.

Before we knew it, the babies were developed enough to be born. I stopped taking the medication that prevented preterm labor and the doctor lifted all restrictions on my activity. When I began retaining fluid, he decided to induce labor. Scheduling the births of our twins turned out to be convenient not only in preventing a middle of the night surprise for John, me, and the medical personnel but also for the film crew, who had to be assembled in advance.

We arrived at the hospital on June 2, and preparations began. My doctor ordered one last ultrasound to confirm the position of the babies before we got started. But before my doctor performed the ultrasound, rumblings of a disagreement in the hallway drifted into earshot. John checked it out and explained that our doctor told the *Primetime* producer he wanted to view the footage before it was processed. The producer explained that it would not be available prior to processing.

Before it was over, the president of the hospital, the chief of obstetrics, and lawyers all around weighed in and ultimately suggested the chief of obstetrics take over the delivery. As if I was not anxious enough with all the emotional and physical strains of the long-anticipated delivery of my children, I now had a perfect stranger, albeit, a highly qualified doctor, in charge of our care. My increasing anxiety and tears set off a parade of people who were quick to assure me everything was fine and that the issues would be resolved. After those reassurances, I calmed down, and we got over hurdle one.

Satisfied with the resolution, my doctor came into the room ready to perform the ultrasound and get started with the induction. As suspected, our son was in good position, but our daughter was head up in the breech position—hurdle two.

For the past several years, there had been a concerted effort to reduce the rate of cesarean births that were not medically indicated, and new regulations put doctors under pressure to continue this trend. So my doctor suggested we go forward with the induction, and should it become medically indicated, he would perform a cesarean section. John would have none of that. His daughter, Laura, was a breech baby, and her delivery was so difficult it had left John with disturbing memories of the pain and chaos that had ensued. Weary of it all and having painful contractions at that point, anything that spelled less work for me got my vote, so I just let John and my doctor battle it out, never doubting who would win.

In fourteen years of administering anesthesia, I had never been present at a multiple birth, and I guess I never thought about the sheer number of people involved. The delivery room took on the air of a three-ring circus. There was my doctor with his scrub and circulating nurses, two complete teams of pediatric support (one for each baby), extra nurses on hand, anesthesia support staff, and ABC's filming crew on top of all that.

The combination of the effects of the epidural, the bright lights, and the drone of conversations swirling around me made everything hazy. My clearest memories were of John holding my hand and talking to me, the anesthesiologist checking for possible problems that might arise, and the commanding voice of my obstetrician, telling John and me how things were progressing.

Then, I heard that first lusty cry of our son, Christian, repeated two minutes later, by our daughter, Meredith, and everything snapped into focus. Our tumultuous five-year journey had finally brought us to this moment, and tears of joy tinged with a little melancholy rolled down my cheeks as I remembered the first cries of the babies who were now gone from my touch. But when the nurse brought Christian over and set him in my arms and I was able to feel his velvety breath on my face, my heart sang a song of thanks and praise for this precious new beginning. John was next to me, holding Meredith, and when our eyes met, we exchanged a look of triumph, with smiles of happiness that felt like they would never fade. The nurse helped us switch babies, and I looked into our daughter's beautiful blue eyes, marveling at the life before me, while John did the same with our son.

John and I were confident parents, but we did not escape the "blur" that becomes the life of moms and dads when they bring a new baby home. We did not have one but two new infants, and yet our family was such a blessed triumph over tragedy that we embraced the additional challenge and maintained a sense of humor through it all. Those first nights rocking the babies, I sang lullabies that I had sung to Dawn, Steven, and Michael, and initially the memories cached in my heart tightened my chest until tears drowned out the melody, but the soft breathing of the baby in my arms would draw me out of yesterday and into tomorrow. From there, each day became a little easier and brighter than the day before. We were truly blessed.

As days turned into months, our babies continued to enrich our lives, our circle of friends grew, and my outlook continued to brighten. I no longer woke up weighed down with sadness; rather, I confidently embraced the day and the many blessings it held.

Now I could have said that my instincts helped me weather the incomprehensible storm that co-opted my life, but with my newfound perspective, I realized instinct alone would never have been enough. It was the tug and pull of the Spirit that led me through that tunnel of darkness to a new sunrise. He gave me the strength to get through the unimaginable, and instead of being satisfied with myself and my happiness, I wanted to inspire others. I wanted to give them hope that no matter how dire the circumstances of our life, we have a faithful God who is Lord of all creation. He abounds in love and mercy and knits together the pieces of shattered lives. I wanted broken hearts to know that when we seek God amid chaos, He answers and lights our path. The path may not be easy, and the direction and timing may not be what we had hoped for, but the answer according to His purpose will *always* be wise and abundant.

HEART OF
THE MATTER

We don't want to miss the blessings of the Lord because they do not arrive in the time frame of our choosing nor in the package we had hoped for. There are times of confusion and despair when waiting seems like torture. But we must remember that God is never late. In our waiting we can plead our case to Him and then place our needs in His capable hands. We can be confident that His plan for us will unfold according to His will and purpose in His perfect timing.

Blessed is the one who waits.

—Daniel 12:12 NIV

It didn't take long for a sharing opportunity to arise. John and I had finally reached a point where we were comfortable leaving the twins for a brief period, so John planned our first post-delivery dinner out. We went to a quaint French restaurant where George, our favorite waiter, greeted us and excitedly asked about the babies. He was doubly excited because another couple with infant twins was dining in the restaurant, and he was anxious to introduce us.

Leah and Stan were terrific. We clicked immediately, especially when discussing our children. They had a young son, Cole, and now twin daughters, Allegra and Siena. That brief first encounter led to a wonderful new friendship as well as opportunities for me to broaden my outreach.

Leah and I began attending a support group for new moms called "Mothers of Multiples." The incidence of complications and death was greater in a multiple pregnancy and birth, and Leah and I came face-to-face with that in our group. We had both been blessed with healthy children, but that was not the case for a number of other families.

With my experience and Leah's compassion, our hearts were moved to reach out to those around us. We created "Multiple Angels," a bereavement support group for parents with losses in multiple births. I devoted a lot of time and effort to Multiple Angels, as it was an outlet for the surrendered grief that had quietly taken up permanent residence in my heart and still bubbled up on occasion to the surface. I knew that speaking with those bereaved parents, hearing their stories, and sharing my journey with them was all part of God's plan for me.

With this new initiative came a new direction. I began a gradual shift away from advocacy for trucking regulations and toward serving the bereaved. There was still plenty to do to keep our highways safe, but I felt a tug toward the victims of tragedy, and Multiple Angels was definitely a way to reach those who needed to be lifted up.

And my love of writing never waned. I continued to write words of encouragement to those in need, as so many had done for me, and I could never forget to thank Dr. Paulson and the team at USC Fertility for their part in making our new family possible.

August 17, 1994

Dear Dr. Paulson,

Where do I begin? For weeks, I have been trying to write to you, trying to put into words the incredible feelings of seeing a true miracle. I will start by tell you that after an uneventful pregnancy, Meredith and Christian Berger were born. Now, eleven weeks later, we still look at these babies and are in awe of the tremendous blessing granted to us.

We want to extend our deepest and most heartfelt thanks to you and your staff for making this miracle possible. Our experience with you was such a positive one right from the start. Everyone was pleasant and caring and created a relaxed atmosphere for us, which really helped us deal with the built-in stress of an IVF cycle. Throughout the cycle, we prayed so ardently for the promise of new life and for all of you, that you would be guided to success in your work. Our prayers were answered twofold! We will be forever grateful to you for your part in the miracle of life.

Our best personal regards to all,

John and Donna

Since the *Primetime Live* segment would highlight the twins' birth and baptism, it took a while before the segment aired. We had planned a special day with about forty family members and friends for the baptism.

When we arrived, however, it turned into something quite different. Pastor Mike's large extended family packed the church. He had told our story during his homily at the Mass just prior to the baptism, and many parishioners stayed on to join in the celebration. We were so blessed to have our babies lifted up by such a large community of Christians praying together. It was awesome to behold.

When the *Primetime* segment finally aired, we received even more attention. Since John and I both grew up in Fairfield County, we knew a lot of people in the area, and many called or stopped us in public to chat. We also received letters from all over, like this one from someone who had been there that devastating August day.

July 12, 1995

Dear Donna,

I was so glad to see you tonight on *Primetime Live*. I've thought about you so many times these past few years. You see, I was there on the Florida Turnpike the day of the accident. I'm still haunted by my memories of that day. I was the tenth car in a line of traffic going north when the traffic stopped. I got out of my car and walked up to where you were. The paramedics were taking care of you. I just couldn't believe what the other bystanders told me. Over the years, I have thought that the story of your family just couldn't be true.

I'm a nurse in Fort Lauderdale, and I travel north frequently to visit my mother in Titusville, Florida. The thought of you and your family breaks my heart every time I drive by that area. I'm so glad to finally have found out that you survived your wounds and have recovered so well. Your children are beautiful. I think it is wonderful that you have fallen in love and have a happy life.

My best wishes to you and your family,

Sincerely,

Roxanne

Several local newspapers and magazines also contacted me for feature interviews. While I appreciated all the interest and support, and I truly wanted to be responsive to everyone, I was fearful of overcommitting. I was a new mother, and I wanted time alone with my new family. We wanted to do the things that families did, like walk through the park together or go out for a family meal, but that had become difficult because John and I were always being recognized in public. When *Primetime* reran the episode six months later, the attention only amplified.

One day, as we shopped at Costco, two complete strangers called out to us, "You're the couple from TV!" at which point heads turned and a small group began to gather around us. We were gracious, but John had had enough, and afterward he said, "We're moving!"

So we began looking for a place to begin our new lives. We needed that fresh start not just for the twins but also for ourselves.

Despite raising two one-year-olds and being in the process of moving, I still did my best to reach out to people in pain whenever the opportunity arose. I wrote to Edye Smith after she lost her two boys in the Oklahoma City bombing, and through Alive Alone, I shared my story with many parents dealing with what I had been through. I also became connected with a group called "Parents Against Tired Truckers (PATT)." PATT, a group advocating for truck safety, was founded by Daphne and Steve Izer after their 16-year-old son Jeffrey and three other passengers in the same car were killed in a tractor-trailer collision. The driver of the rig had fallen asleep at the wheel, drifted off the roadway, and crashed into Jeffrey's parked car. Through this wonderful group, I was able to reach out to many more victims.

I found myself drawn to those struggling with the loss of a child or children and the decision of whether to have more. I recognized everyone was different, and I understood the perpetual fear of another tragedy striking those closest to them that stuck in the corner of their minds, but I also knew how I felt about my twins. I would rather have had Dawn, Stephen, and Michael, and now, Christian and Meredith, for the time God gave them to me, however short, than not at all.

I knew in my heart that I had wanted more children because I loved being a mom. It wasn't to replace Dawn, Stephen, and Michael in my heart. I also wanted John and me to share that emotional bond of parenthood.

I met some mothers who tried to keep their deceased children alive through the ones that followed. Every moment of every day would be a remembrance, and as much as I wanted Christian and Meredith to know their big sister and brothers, I felt that was not the best approach for John and me or our twins. I did not want Meredith and Christian's home to be a place where they felt they had to compete for my love and approval with the dreams and memories, however precious, of a family and a lifetime that no longer existed.

Honestly, it was too painful and sapped too much energy to honor Dawn, Stephen, and Michael's memories at all times. Moderation became the key. I did not want to deny their memories, but I couldn't keep their personal items and pictures all over the house. I didn't want to turn our home into a shrine. I didn't think they would want that either. Moreover, it would be too hard to live in the present and be there for Christian and Meredith if I was constantly revisiting the past. I wasn't sure if that was right or wrong—or if there even *was* a correct answer—but it felt healthy and right for me. I accepted the fact of the unjust tragedy that hit my family and me, and I needed to move forward and learn how to go back on my own terms to visit when necessary, when my heart called me.

For these reasons and others, I decided to share with Alive Alone how I felt on the seven-year anniversary of the crash.

Dear Dawn, Stephen, Michael, and Gerry (Daddy),

It seems impossible that it's been seven years since I've seen your smiling faces, held your hands, wiped away a tear, or given you a good-night kiss. It seems like yesterday we were all together, traveling down the Florida Turnpike, so happy and excited about going on vacation. Then, in a heartbeat, all of you were gone. As I sat in the middle of the highway, burned and dazed, I realized that all that was left of our beautiful family were the ashes on my hands.

The pain of losing all of you has been almost beyond endurance. For the first two years, I could not get through a single day without what seemed like endless sorrow that reduced me to tears. I cried until I had no more tears left. Then, gradually, I began letting my memories of each of you take on a new perspective. You were such happy children. Beautiful, strong, and determined, always ready to embrace life to its fullest. Your dad and I loved you so very much, and you all returned that love many times over, as only children can do. You were such a team, always loving, caring, and watching out for each other. Even when you argued, one of you could usually come up with a reluctant "sorry" to end the match and make up. Gerry, you were a kind, considerate, and loving husband and father.

As I looked back on all these memories, I realized I needed to celebrate and honor each of your lives. The best way I figured I could do this was by building a new life for myself and making you proud of your mom. Over the years, I have done many things in your honor. There is a beautiful stained-glass window of the tree of life and a flowering garden at your school. I have worked tirelessly to improve highway safety, and I run a group for moms and dads who have lost children.

I married "Uncle" John, and your friend Laura is now your stepsister. I know how much all of you wanted another baby. You, in particular, Dawn, wanted a sister. Well, two years ago, we had twins! You have a sister, Meredith, who is very much like you, Dawn. She has your spirit and those beautiful blue eyes. You also have a brother named Christian. Everyone says he looks a lot like you, Michael, but his personality is more like yours, Stephen. John and I have a wonderful life with Laura and the twins. And all of you will forever be a part of it.

Often, I think back on our life together, and I remember with a smile and a tear the busy but fun times. Dawn, I miss your energy, your can-do personality, our "girl" talks, your diligence when it came to school and projects, your "borrowing" my sweaters and rolling up the sleeves, the endless hours in skating rinks everywhere, last-minute touches to your skating outfits and your hair, but, most of all, I miss that mother/daughter friendship we shared.

Stephen, I miss hockey and T-ball and all your friends' calls asking if you could come play, but, most of all, I miss your humor, that sunny smile, and those tight hugs followed by your kisses.

Michael, you were such a beautiful and sweet child; how did you ever get into all the mischief you did? I miss all the funny things you did, like having to hunt for your blanket and trying to find those two "guys," which were invariably lost right at bedtime.

Gerry, my friend and partner in this beautiful but unfinished symphony, I miss what we had and what never came to be, but I am forever grateful for what was.

I will always love and miss all of you, and I live with a quiet yet undeniable longing for you and that part of my heart you took with you when you left. But I have come to understand and accept that each of you are safe and happy in heaven with the Lord. We all rejoice for you in your new "life" and look forward to that time when our spirits will be together again.

Love,

Mom

I had to find a quiet day with complete privacy in my closet of memories and go back seven years into the archives of life to write that letter. Every fiber of my being trembled, and I sobbed as I wrote to my beloved family, now beyond my touch. When I was done, I was exhausted but filled with a gentle peace. My acceptance prevented the seeds of bitterness from taking root in my heart and instead afforded me strength and resilience.

We finally moved and our children were growing up healthy and happy. After recovering from the move, I was able to get more involved in Multiple Angels. Leah and I felt we were providing an important service for many in need. I was given an opportunity to reach even more people when *Woman's Day* magazine contacted me about telling my story.

I realized after the article came out that Christian and Meredith were three years old, the same age Michael was when he died. There was a sadness in recognizing that the twins had now reached an age that Michael had never lived beyond. I was not sad that Christian and Meredith were growing up; every day I thanked the Lord for each of my children and for every moment I got to spend with them. Rather, I was sad thinking that Michael would have been eleven years old. Stephen would have been fourteen, and Dawn would have been seventeen and about to graduate from high school. Dawn, Stephen, and Michael would never reach those ages, and I would never get to share in all those memories. Not spending that lifetime with my children broke my heart, but I reminded myself they were rejoicing in the love of the Lord, and I pictured their smiling faces, which brought a smile to mine.

It seemed life would be smooth sailing from here on. We were preparing for our first Christmas together in our new house, and we were counting our blessings every day. I was so relieved to have finally gotten over my mountain, to have finally chiseled down to that final pebble, the one I put in my pocket and would carry with me forever. Never would I face anything remotely as challenging ever again . . . or so I thought.

CHAPTER 13

Saved by Grace through Faith

I will give thanks to the LORD with my whole heart;
I will recount all of your wonderful deeds.

—Psalm 9:1 ESV

I rode a wave of peace and calm through a grace-filled season. Grief no longer pushed me off-balance at every turn. God sat on the throne of my heart, where I trusted Him and passed the decisions in my life under the light of His truth. But, eventually, I drifted into the busyness of everyday life, and I didn't always stop to pray, listen, and seek His counsel. I would not say that I edged God off the throne of my heart, but while concentrating on raising two young children in a new home and a new community, there was so much to do and so many decisions to make that I lost focus. Rather than unseating God, I gradually, almost imperceptibly, began the climb to sit up there next to Him.

The twins began school, and the parent-volunteer opportunities were fulfilling. They allowed me to be involved in the children's time away from home and helped fill the void that being unable to return to my career had created. Volunteering also led me to a great group of new friends and introduced me to the many wonderful aspects of our new community.

Sometimes, it was awkward. In an attempt to be friendly, people would ask questions, but I did not want to divulge too much of my past. Partly, I did not want people to pity me as the woman who had lost her family, but more than that, I wanted to shelter my children. I did not want people to treat our family, especially the children, differently. John and I wanted to provide them with the best childhood we could, and we could not focus on the future if we continued to step back into the past.

HEART OF THE MATTER

Our past can tend to hold us captive. Ideally, we need to work through it. But if we can't work through it fully, as is often the case in grief, we need to outfit it with an on/off switch. If we are to step into the future, we must have hope and faith that there is a future to step into that the past will not trample on.

> Weeping may last through the night,
> but joy comes with the morning.
>
> —Psalm 30:5 NLT

That choice to distance myself from my past at times played a part in me being pulled away from my closeness with the Lord and the faith that had seen me through my most desperate times. In my attempt to move forward, I tended to stay on the corner of "easy" and "happy."

At times I lost sight of the many ways in which I needed the Lord in order to simply survive, but that whisper in my heart drew me back, giving me strength and guidance to regain my center. Caring for my family was the right thing, and even volunteering was a service to the children, their parents, and the school. Yet I knew the Lord did not necessarily want me to *do* more but to *be* more in Him. I had a unique opportunity in the wake of the crash to draw close to the Lord, and I did not want to drift away from that relationship, although that was precisely what I was in danger of doing.

In his book, James says to count trials as joy (see James 1:2 KJV). We don't count them for the hardship they cause but for fact that they bring us closer to God and edify our faith. I found that to be so true.

I also found that the more I clung to the Lord, like Job, the harder the enemy worked to pull us apart. When a close doctor friend asked us to participate in an orientation for a new heart scanner at his hospital, John and I signed up along with several friends to be guinea pigs. My results were normal, but when three days went by and we had not heard from Scott about John's scan, I grew concerned.

Finally, I called him up and asked, "Scott, what's going on?"

With my medical background, thoughts of coronary artery disease and blockages filled my head. Never did I suspect what Scott was about to tell me. When John saw my eyes fill with tears as I listened to the explanation of the results, he poured himself a glass of vodka.

"What are you doing?" I asked, distraught from the phone call I had just completed.

"I figured the way you were crying, I must be on my way out, so why not?" John said.

Despite the humor, the tears poured down as I tried to pull myself together and relay the results. Scott had told me he spent several sleepless nights of worry over how to break the news to John. He had also used the time to gather information and specialists to contact. John had a congenital malformation of his heart known to cause sudden death in otherwise healthy athletes such as "Pistol" Pete Maravich. It explained why John had passed out several times during his football career, but his condition was so obscure that it had always been attributed to heat exhaustion.

We entered another of life's trials that held the potential to strengthen or challenge our faith. And so began the odyssey to figure out what the future might hold. As for us, we drew closer to the Lord, praying for wisdom and direction. The journey was not always smooth or timely, but we got opinions from New York to California and even as far away as a specialist in Italy. Ultimately, we ended up at Yale New Haven Hospital and took the advice of a senior cardiologist there who shared our faith. It puzzled the doctors how John could have ever played football and worked out as hard as he did in the martial arts with his heart defect. But he did, and since he had no symptoms, there was nothing to be done. The cardiologist urged him to take some exercise precautions, but, otherwise, he told John to put this behind him and live his life. He also assured me that if a problem arose, John would have symptoms to alert us.

As if the events of my life had not made it clear enough, I remembered again just how measured our time on this earth was. It appeared John would be okay. We were blessed and I was so thankful. The Lord reigned on the throne of my life, and more than anything, I wanted Him there forever.

Life continued to pull me in many different directions, but I was determined to strike a balance. Although I did not live in the past, the past lived in me and in the person I had become. There was no getting around the limitations of my hands, how fragile my skin was, or how sensitive I was to the harsh, cold weather of New England. And, while I had traveled through the early and middle rigors of grief, the death of a child remained an irreconcilable loss. As the years passed, I had learned how to live with my "shadow" grief, but it was not something I shared with anyone but God.

I wanted to live more in the present joy where John and our children abided, and yet, that spirituality I craved had come only when everything was crumbling around me. Having known the peace of abiding in Jesus made the busyness of life seem petty and annoying at times. But, then again, the enemy excels at the petty and annoying, distracting us from walking in faith.

While John and the children were always my first priority, the allure and glitz of suburban living kept beckoning. Through it all, that inner voice was a guiding light. I felt like I was doing so many things that I could not catch my breath, and I felt that I was not doing any of them well. On the outside, I was like supermom, but on the inside, I was feeling defeated and insecure about who I was and how I was living my life. To maintain balance would mean sacrificing some of the world around me and maybe even revisiting some of the twists and turns in the road I had already traveled. This would mean not being on so many boards and committees and saying no to some events and trips. It also meant I would probably lose some of the friendships I had formed.

It had been no easy task to climb down from the throne and leave my life and its direction to God, and maybe that was what Elisabeth meant when she had said that the further along we are in our spirituality, the harder the road gets. I realized that the closer we draw to the Lord, the greater the hurdles and stumbling blocks the enemy throws our way to trip us up. But I knew that if I put my trust in God, He would come up with a solution for me. I waited and prayed I would not miss any opportunities set before me, and when the call came out for a bereavement counselor at our church, I applied and was welcomed into that ministry.

I passed up a few volunteer opportunities and missed some lunches, but every minute spent for God was so edifying. Throughout the years I worked as a bereavement counselor, I met and liked to think I brought God's comfort to many hurting people. Most of them were older, widows and widowers struggling with the loss of their lifelong spouses, and it was my blessing to share any pearls of wisdom on healing and moving forward that I had gleaned from my personal journey through grief.

By this time, the twins had reached and passed both Stephen and Dawn's ages, and it was particularly hard when they passed Dawn's. The days of using the twins' age as a reference point for memories of Dawn, Stephen, and Michael had come to an end, and while it truly was a new and exciting time with the twins, for the first time in my life, I had children who were nine years old. Each day was a wonderful adventure with Meredith and Christian, but, at the same time, I was saddened to think that my first three children would never reach their age and beyond.

With memories of the past lurking in the recesses of my mind, I often had difficulty letting go as Christian and Meredith grew up. If they were at a friend's house for a sleepover, my imagination would run wild, and I would think the house might catch fire or some other disaster would strike.

One summer day, I hastily told John not to forget the twins were in the pool as I rushed out the door to drive to a meeting. He was upset over a disagreement we had and did not respond, and as I drove, the anxiety began to build. *What if he did not hear me? What if he did not take me seriously? What if the twins were in trouble?*

By the time I reached my destination, I was having a full-blown panic attack and had to turn around and drive home to make sure they were safe. As I pulled into the driveway, I could see John sitting by the pool, keeping a watchful eye on them. Overcoming that persistent fear of something happening to my children, particularly when they were away from us, was one of my greatest challenges at that time. I rationalized it all day long and then tried to hand it over to God, but it took years for the Lord to coax that fear from my clenched fingers.

With everything God had done for me, it should have been easy to put all my trust in Him. He had rebuilt my life far beyond what I could have ever dreamed possible. When I thought about the past decade, I was ever so thankful for the gift of faith that got me through the most difficult journey of my life and revealed the fruits He had in store for me on the other side.

Without that biblical "mustard seed," I might have turned away from God, but that did not happen. I believed that when the accident occurred, God said, "She's mine," and the power and provisions of heaven rained down, keeping me alive. Since then, He carefully knit together the broken pieces of my life. But I yearned for more. I wanted that steadfast personal relationship that God is passionate about for each of us.

How often do we miss what is right before us? God had been there the entire time. He sat on the burning pavement with me at the site of the accident. He held my hand through the unrelenting pain in the burn unit. He collected all my tears through years of grief. He held me close in John's love and smiled at me through the faces of my children. God had always been in my head, and He was a faithful presence in my life. His Holy Spirit had carried me through those tough years, comforting and guiding me. *I* was the one who didn't know how to really be in a relationship with God. No longer was I satisfied to *know about* Him, I wanted to fully *know and experience* Him. I wanted to praise Him, honor Him and serve Him. I wanted to live a life of gratitude and humility.

Truthfully, since the twins had been born, my faith had gradually become more of an obligation than a passion. I had a taste of what a loving, spiritual relationship with God could be, and I wanted that heart relationship forever. I continued to pray for the Lord to reveal the next part of His plan for me, and once again, I found His answer in the unexpected. There is an often-used saying: When the student is ready, the teacher will appear. I was finally ready.

One hot August day, we headed to Dreams Park in Cooperstown, New York, where John was coaching in a baseball tournament. It was an exciting week for our team, and the boys ended up playing in the quarterfinal game after five days of pool play. The entire trip was an amazing experience, but, sadly, the day before that game, we received an incredibly difficult call. It was a call from our friend Father Fred, letting us know that our dear friend, Lucille, had passed away that morning. Her cancer had spread to her lungs, and on my last visit, she only had the strength to smile as I held her hand and talked to her. I knew the end was near, and while I was thankful for the seven wonderful years we had together, her passing was heartbreaking.

Christian said he was going to get a hit for Lucille in that quarterfinal game, and he delivered with an important double that brought bittersweet tears to my eyes. We all grieved the loss of our dear friend. We so enjoyed our friendship with Lucille and her family over the years, and it was truly a blessing and an honor to be a part of the final chapter of Lucille's life.

As often happens with sports teams, parents bonded, and this trip was no exception. That morning, before game time, one of the moms had asked me if I would like to walk with her. During that hour-long walk, Annesley invited me to join her Bible study. A teacher appeared just when I was ready to take the next step in my relationship with God. It was not as earth-shattering as the angel Gabriel appearing to Daniel when he prayed, but God's handprint was all over it.

During that study, I was transformed. The Lord was no longer ink on a page but a loving Father who was embracing me in that personal relationship for which I thirsted. I knew where I wanted to be, but being in His Word was a brand-new navigation system that showed me how to get there.

Pastor Neely Towe led that study of the books of Samuel. She had a heart for David in the Old Testament and a gift for bringing him and every aspect of his relationship with God to life.

The Bible said that David was a man after God's own heart, and his example of mourning resonated with me. In 1 Samuel, when David and his men came back from battle and found their wives and children had been abducted, they cried out and wept until they had no more strength to weep. Again, in 2 Samuel, David publicly lamented his personal grief over the death of Saul and his close friend, Jonathan. It affirmed for me that we *should* cry out to the Lord when we were suffering, and I was right in doing so after the accident. As Pastor Towe explained, lamenting was a cry of belief in God, because life mattered to God, and senseless loss of life mattered to God because He created life. God was not absent; He was there with David in his grief just like He was with me in mine, and we needed to lament, because if we tried to handle it on our own, our grief could separate us from God.

I was ever so grateful for the Spirit's comfort and guidance in my life, particularly during those dark nights of my soul so many years ago.

Through the study, I was reintroduced to the Spirit of God within and the endless ways He works powerfully in our lives. I also learned how to pray in a whole new way, bowing down with a repentant heart before the Lord in praise and thanksgiving and with confidence in His faithfulness. My prayer life became a whole new window into my relationship with the Lord.

Another aspect of that Bible study that I so loved was the way this group of Christian women was able to converse and nurture each other so well. The fellowship in this group of women was free from the everyday carping and complaints that often dominates small talk. It was not exclusively non-secular; it was more of a secular relationship infused with the spiritual, and while some of my fears about losing friends came true as I left some of my former endeavors and volunteer positions, I found that relationships with these new friends were rich and satisfying. When I would meet my fellow Bible study members in the grocery store or on the ball field, there was a bond we had that brought a distinct blessing to our conversations. They enabled me to bring a brighter and more positive perspective to my many wonderful friendships outside of the group as well.

This experience lit up my soul, and I felt more connected to the Lord than ever before. The time I devoted to being with God in His Word led me to a far greater appreciation of the amazing gifts He gave me in the years after the crash. It took heartfelt desire and dedication to have that sort of relationship with God, particularly in the secular world in which we lived, but I loved every minute of it. I was ever so grateful for the grace that enables faith, which I considered my greatest gift from the Lord as I began this journey lying in a lonely hospital bed. I could see now that while I had been asking for "bread" and feeling like I was getting "stones," God had been giving me the Bread of Heaven, which was far more fulfilling. Seemingly unanswered prayers had been confusing and disappointing, but God had used those pauses to draw me closer to Him and grow my faith.

As Ephesians 3:20 states, "[T]hrough His mighty power at work within [me], [He] accomplish[ed] infinitely more than [I] might ask or think."

I not only had my prayers answered and receive the most precious gifts I could desire but I also received the added joy of celebrating it all in communion with Him. This was only made possible by the time of testing in which He showed me that "I can do everything through Christ, who gives me strength" (Phil. 4:13 NLT).

Leaning on Christ was the only way to navigate the highway of life which was filled with twists and turns, and it wasn't long before the next turn. My mother, who was in a nursing home, was not doing well. She had been battling Alzheimer's disease for over a decade now, and her nurse called to tell me it looked like she might pass away at any moment, but she thought my mom might be waiting for me.

Mom was semicomatose when I arrived at her bedside and reached for her hand. Everything I had learned from Elisabeth, from my reading on death, faith, the afterlife, and my Bible study did not fail me. It all served to strengthen me in that moment, and with the direction of the Spirit within, I was able to pray with confidence over my mother for her safe passage.

"It's okay, Mom," I told her. "We're all okay. You can let go . . . Jesus is waiting for you."

As she was close to death, it was difficult to tell if what I was saying got through to my mother or not, but something inside me knew that it had. Early the next morning, I got another call saying that my mother was at peace.

While she had not been herself for years, it still was not easy to lose my only living parent. There was a comfort, even as adults, in the parent-child connection, and that comfort was now gone. The only parent I had left to lean on was my Father in heaven, but a blessing of life was the realization that He was all I ever truly needed. I had faith that God loved me, and that despite trials and sorrows, one day when I was looking back in time, I would see the beautiful tapestry of my life that He had woven together. I would see how very present He was in watching over me and guiding me through it all—every step of the way.

A lot of people over the years had expressed disbelief at how I was able to continue my life after what had happened. I had lost everything—my husband, my children, my job, my community, my self-image, and, for one dark moment, my spirit—at that point, the tapestry of my life had unraveled into a tragedy that most people had never experienced and would consider beyond recovery from. My friend and attorney, Chris Searcy, had compared me to a "phoenix arising from the ashes," referring to the mythological creature that would suddenly burst into flames, burn down to only ashes, and then rise out of the ashes, reborn. The *Woman's Day* article written about me had been entitled "Rising from the Ashes." With my life literally and figuratively burning up in an instant, I guess it was an appropriate comparison.

But I was *not* the phoenix. I shared the obvious similarities and had recovered against what many considered impossible odds, but unlike the phoenix, I was not my own savior. Jesus Christ gave me life again. Without Him, I know I would not have survived, and enduring the horrors I did made it clear to me that Jesus's promises were true. But my Redeemer did not come to save me alone, He came to save the world. No matter what we do or what others do to us, God is loving and faithful to those who believe in Him and abide in Him, living according to His Word and His expectations of us in this life.

HEART OF THE MATTER

Jesus's love healed my broken heart. And while a healed heart bears the scars of the trials and tragedies it has been through, those scars do not create the path of our future. The Lord creates beauty out of our ashes, and His sacrifice brings us redemption and the promise of eternal life. Daily, He is the reason to live without ever losing hope for tomorrow.

Do not be afraid or discouraged, for the Lord will
personally go ahead of you. He will be with you;
He will neither fail you nor abandon you.

—Deuteronomy 31:8

Epilogue

This hope is a strong and trustworthy anchor for our souls.
It leads us through the curtain into God's inner sanctuary.

—HEBREWS 6:19

Charlottesville, Virginia—Fall 2012

It occurred to me that this was a special place to return to. The last time I had flown into the airport here, I was on my way to Dr. Elisabeth Kübler-Ross's workshop, which gave impetus to the healing and peace that preceded my present visit. This time, I was staying in Charlottesville rather than busing to Head Waters, because Meredith, the daughter I would not have been able to have without the strength and courage I gained years before, was a first-year student at the University of Virginia. Chris Searcy, who is a UVA alumnus, welcomed us as guests in his home on the grounds of the University.

As we warmed ourselves by the fire pit in the back yard, we reminisced over the passing years. Perhaps it was the bittersweet nature of the recollections we shared that prompted Chris to begin telling us a story we had never heard.

"You know, at the time, I didn't really know if I should tell you or not," Chris said in his slow Southern drawl. "I figured it was just as well if I didn't talk to you about the things you didn't remember. But it's something that's stuck with me."

He paused and then looked to us.

"Do you remember those witnesses who came forward at the last minute?"

John and I looked at each other and shook our heads, indicating we did not.

"Carlyle? Kyle and Kim Carlyle? They were the ones who were driving behind the tractor-trailer and watched it drift off the road and into the emergency lane."

John and I then nodded in awareness, although we had never met them in person.

"Well, I met with the wife, Kim, and she asked if she could tell me something off the record. I said, 'Sure,' so she started talking about the man who had helped Donna at the scene of the crash, describing him in great detail. She was so impressed by his calming effect on Donna that she wanted to thank him for his compassion.

"When the paramedics arrived, he stood and began to walk through the circle of onlookers behind him. Kim followed. But she couldn't find him anywhere. It was as if he had just vanished.

"I think she believes she saw an angel and that God had sent that angel down from heaven to watch over Donna until help arrived."

We sat in silence. Somehow, it all strangely made sense. God had been there for me throughout my entire life, and He had carried me through the most difficult times. Whether this was truly His angel or someone who had been Spirit-led, I believed that it was yet another gift from God. Another piece of my life that clicked into place.

"Anyway, it seemed to spook Kim, which is why she didn't talk to us until years later," Chris said. "I guess she was afraid people would think she was crazy . . .

"But ever since I heard her description of the angel, I always thought it sounded like John."

Laughing, John said, "Trust me, Chris, I'm no angel."

"Well, you were in Connecticut at the time, so it couldn't have been you," Chris said with a shrug. "But it still struck me as a spot-on description of what you looked like."

John took a deep breath before continuing.

"You know, Chris, it's kind of interesting you brought this up. Because Donna and I had a similar experience about a year and a half after the accident.

"We were in New York, and Donna takes off into a crowded intersection. I mean, right into traffic, and I'm standing there watching her and thinking, *This is it. She's dead.* But somehow, she makes it across. When I reached her, my heart was pounding, and I asked her what the heck she was thinking."

"And what did she say?" asked Chris.

"Very calmly, she tells me 'I wasn't alone, there was that guy next to me. He was tall, broad-shouldered, had light brown hair, maybe blond or red . . . and do you know who he kind of looked like?'"

"Who?"

"*You!*" John exclaimed. "I'm telling you, Chris, there wasn't anybody there, but she said there was this big guy there blocking all the traffic and that he kind of looked like *you.*"

Chris smiled, though a tear was in his eye.

"Isn't that something?" he said.

Through the years, there were many milestones and memories. Some of the milestones we marked continued to cast a shadow of grief. For many Christmases, it was bittersweet to sit down to dinner with everyone after all the preparations were finally finished and to feel that emptiness. I would look around and seldom say anything. But not seeing Gerry, Dawn, Stephen, and Michael's smiling faces tugged at my heart.

Christian and Meredith's high school graduation had been difficult as well. My tears of joy over this rite of passage and how grown up the twins were mixed together with thoughts of what could have also been with my other children. They missed their high school graduation and a lifetime more.

All my friends were having grandchildren, and while I was truly happy for them and to see their pictures, videos, and comments on social media, I yearned to know what my grandchildren would have been like. Dawn and Stephen would most likely have had children of their own by now, and I grew teary thinking about all we had missed out on.

Thankfully, the grace of the Holy Spirit allowed me to redirect my sight on the faithfulness of the Lord in my life. I believed in my heart that my family was in a better place, and while that did not change the awful circumstances of their deaths, the important fact was that they were with God, and that brought me great peace. In believing that, I knew I did not have to hold on to them so tightly anymore. Letting go wasn't a sign of betrayal or weakness. Nor did it mean I gave up. It meant I had gained the strength I needed to reach the point of accepting the unimaginable. Once I did that, I was able to surrender my life to the Lord, freeing myself to live and love again without worry or regret.

A large part of my ability to let go—my acceptance—came from learning that without forgiveness, there could not be acceptance, and without acceptance, a grieving heart could not heal. The difficult part is that we are called to forgive even if the person who hurt us does not ask for or deserve our forgiveness.

Jesus forgave the undeserving and that is what He calls on us to do. It doesn't happen overnight, but when we finally use that key of forgiveness to let ourselves out of our prisons of sadness, anger, and bitterness, we are filled with grace, and we experience the exhilarating freedom to live the abundant life that God has created for us.

HEART OF THE MATTER

Forgiving is not about the person we are forgiving; it's about healing our own heart. We do not condone the actions that hurt us, although we have to accept that forgiveness doesn't mean that the person who hurt us will change. But in forgiving, it is us who are changed, and as we are battered by the storms of life, in forgiving we often discover the man or woman that God intended us to be.

Forgiveness, in turn, births acceptance. The truth is, we never get over the loss of our loved ones. But only in accepting it are we able to live with our loss. And only in acceptance can we celebrate that our loved ones are rejoicing with Jesus in resurrection glory. In acceptance we allow the Lord to be the One to write the story of our tomorrows.

We do not "grieve as others do who have no hope."

—1 Thessalonians 4:13 ESV

I have often said I would always miss that piece of my heart that Gerry and the kids took with them, and that is as true as ever, but each new child showed me the amazing propensity of the human heart to love both infinitely and completely. I could focus on the new love I had gained while still being able to revisit the gentle placeholders of my heart that served as cherished photos in the album of my life. This is not to say that there were not moments in time that launched me back into the intense grief of those first few years, but, more often than not, I could smile at the memory of good times and continue forward into the future. There I could look over my shoulder and see how skillfully God had knitted together the shattered pieces of my life.

Ever since Chris told me the story of the angel that comforted me during the accident, I could not get it out of my mind. Was it an example of how God had been walking with me my entire life and another reason why I should never lose hope? Hebrews 1:14 tells us "angels are ministering spirits sent to care for the people who will inherit salvation." Could it be that on several occasions, I had witnessed a physical form of one of God's angels? Whether that was true or not, I took it as another sign of God's goodness and faithful presence in my life. God was my loving Father who had been there through it all, even during the times I didn't acknowledge His presence right there beside me.

The more I experienced the epiphanies of life such as this, the clearer the meaning of life became. We learn to walk in the ways of the Lord of all creation so He will help us weather the storms and withstand the temptations of our earthly life.

If we hold on tightly to our faith, trusting in the Lord in all things—even when we fall short—we will find Him waiting for us at the gates of eternity with open arms.

I understand how taking up the Cross of Christ is not always easy, and I know how badly this world can batter us. We may feel that we may never be happy again. We carry a lot of baggage and our journey is difficult. But I am living proof that we can make it. I, too, have cried until I had no more tears, but I now realize that living a "zombie existence" is unacceptable. I've also learned that we can live again. Joy exists for us—it is waiting to be found in the Lord.

At the end of the day, faith built from the gift of God's grace is our choice to accept. And yes: for me, it most definitely *was* a challenge. Even as things continued to weigh me down, it meant waking up every day and praying, "Lord, I love You. Let me be your servant. Fill me with your Spirit and guide me to your purpose." Allowing the Lord to prioritize the day was a surrender that set me free, and as I grew older and stronger in my relationship with Christ, any sense of obligation toward His will was replaced with a fervent love of the Lord and a heartfelt desire to follow Him all day, every day.

Those were the lessons I learned through my sometimes very difficult life, and those were the lessons I wanted to share with the people around me and especially pass along to my children. The Lord has given us the tools to gain eternal life, right here amidst the vagaries of our earthly existence. We are called to love, trust, and rely on our faith in our creator. Because as it is written in Esther 4:14, "And who knows whether you have not come to the kingdom for such a time as this?"

God creates every life for a purpose, and we need to be prepared and willing to step up when our time is called. You never know what open door God places before you until you take the time to pray for clarity and open your heart to His guidance. The simplest things, like cooking dinner for your family or volunteering to carpool with an overburdened neighbor, could be an irreplaceable link in the chain of succession that leads to God's plan unfolding in their life or yours.

It is easy to get lost in the tangle of life's daily necessities until the years slip through your fingers. When we look back and say, "Where did the time go?" perhaps what's more important is that we embrace God's purpose for us in the time that is coming.

Perhaps that was why I agreed to take over that Bible study when our leader stepped down. I felt my lack of experience in leading made me far from the best choice, but I also recognized that we cannot be complacent in this life. Sometimes, we have to move out of our comfort zone to grow, and what if it was my time to step up?

Still, apprehension clouded my mind for weeks as I anticipated leading others on a spiritual journey. Doubt followed me on my daily walks with John, when I went out to dinner, and even at the checkout line at the grocery store. I always wanted to do more with my life. I thought often about writing this book, and then I stared down the open door of leading a Bible study. As much as my heart ached to seize those opportunities, the chains of fear held me back. Like Moses, I wanted to say "Lord, are you sure you mean *me*? You know that public speaking is not one of my strengths. What if I'm terrible at it?"

One day, as I was checking out in the express lane at Publix with thoughts such as these on my mind, I sensed a presence. It was that hair-raising feeling on the back of my neck that someone or *something* was watching me.

I slowly turned and found myself gazing up at a very tall young man with light brown, almost reddish hair, in line close behind me. He had a half-smile on his face, and neither of us nodded nor spoke, but when my eyes met his, I was awed by a Spirit-filled moment of grace and affirmation that flooded my senses. Truly, if they were the windows to the soul, his crystal-blue eyes were ethereal.

Instantly, I felt that this was the angel I had encountered twice before. I believed God had used him to guide me, but never before had I seen him face-to-face and recognized just who he was. This time, I did, and it felt as if he had a message to deliver. His smile was affirming, like he was encouraging me without words to keep going forward. It felt as though he had been following me around watching what I was doing, and he was urging me on. Without saying anything, I turned back, gathered my grocery bags, and walked out to my car.

As I made my way through the parking lot, I regretted not trying to communicate with this messenger, but, in my heart, I knew I had received all that I needed.

HEART OF
THE MATTER

My life's journey was not over, and, my friend, your life's journey is not over either. In some ways, I felt it was just beginning, because if God created me "for such a time as this," then I would be just starting out on a long, important stretch of road. I believe the same is true for you. God has created you for such a time as this. I pray we keep our hearts open to the path that God is clearing before us. I pray we are strong in the Lord. I pray each of us will one day be able to stand before God and say,

I have fought the good fight, I have finished the race,
and I have remained faithful.

—2 TIMOTHY 4:7 NLT

I pray that this story of God in my life will touch your hearts and lead you to abide in Him always.

Acknowledgments

From Donna

My utmost praise and thanks go to my Lord and Savior, Jesus Christ, for the courage and the strength to witness to His faithful presence in my life.

My story of love and healing and hope began when God assigned the role of the leading man. I am eternally grateful for my husband, John, who has been by my side from day one, who lifted me up when I could not stand, and who made me laugh through my tears.

John, I would not have made it without you. And this book would never have been possible without your patience, understanding, and support. You tolerated countless hours of solitude while I worked on this project, and I know that readers who find comfort and hope in our story join me in thanking you for your part in making it possible. I love you always and forever.

To our children, Christian, Meredith, and Laura: Your lives breathed healing and purpose back into mine. Together you created a hope for a future that only you could have given me and provided the impetus for me to pay that hope forward. You are living proof that all things are possible when we believe.

There is no way to survive the tragedies of life without God-breathed "angel armies" to lift us up and encourage us through sorrow into healing. Angels like my sister, Nanci; my brother Michael; my sister-in-law Jody; my cousin and soul-sister Madeline; my dear friends Donna Diaz; Jane O'Reilly; Dr. Don

Drew; Janie Drew; Dr. Alberto Guinazu; Dr. Robert Perrotta, Esq.; Lenny Fabrizi; and countless other family members and friends—you know who you are. All of you were an integral part of my survival and recovery, and for that I am eternally grateful.

I am deeply indebted to my attorney and dear friend Christian D. Searcy, Esq. for his profound compassion and care in helping me get through a tragic time in my life. Chris and his team at Searcy Law worked endless hours on my behalf, became like family in the process, and remain so to this day.

I believe that the Lord's hand put Will Searcy in my life at the exact time I was meant to begin this book. We met weekly for two years as we laughed, cried, wrote, *re*wrote, and edited page after page. Will incorporated his own journey through grief into his work as he spent the last days and passing of his precious and beloved mom (and my dear friend), Priscilla Searcy. Priscilla passed away shortly after *Living through Loss* was finished, but her spirit lives on in its mission to bring love, healing, and hope to others.

Sincere gratitude to the wonderful Staff of Shands Burn Center at the University of Florida. Without your individualized care and compassion I would not be here.

After all kinds of grief, but especially after cumulative grief, we need a skilled and compassionate person to guide us through the hurricane of emotions that assail us. God provided me with another angel for that task, Dr. Robert Matefy, PhD.

For almost three years, Bob journeyed with me through my grief. He helped me to come to terms with the agonizing pain (both physical and emotional) and provided me with the coping mechanisms I needed to get through each day . . . or even hour.

He gently cleared a path before me by enabling me to anticipate what I might encounter in my sorrow and depression.

Bob, you will always hold a special place in my heart for your empathy, your friendship, and for your kind and caring spirit. You provided me with an oasis of comfort and rest when I needed it most.

My warmest regards and thanks to Rev. Michael Boccaccio for his guidance and support in celebrating our marriage and in baptizing Meredith and Christian.

Heartfelt thanks to Dr. Richard Paulson and the miracle workers at USC Fertility for the teamwork that made our dream come true.

My thanks as well to Kay and Rodney Bevington of Alive Alone: You came into my life at a time when I needed you most and gave me a support group of parents like myself who were alive, alone. You are true heroes for the work you do in memory of your precious daughter, Rhonda.

To Dr. Judianne Densen-Gerber (1934–2003): Judianne, thank you for starting from the beginning. Your knowledge and amazing insights made all the difference in coping with and recovering from PTSD.

To Dr. Elisabeth Kübler-Ross (1926–2004): Elisabeth, thank you for our personal notes and your encouragement. Your empathy and deep understanding of the grief process gave me the courage to take the next step, and that made all the difference.

My continual thanks, love, and appreciation to Rev. Fred Riendeau. Father Fred has been a dear friend over the years, sharing holidays with us, celebrating Mass in our home, and giving Meredith and Christian their first Holy Communion.

Father Fred has continued to support and encourage my work on *Living through Loss*, and contributes to the design of our website and weekly emails.

To all of my precious Sisters in Faith (SIF), past and present: You have loved, supported and encouraged me throughout this journey. I am grateful beyond measure for each of you and for your praying without ceasing to bring this story of God in my life to those who need it.

Behind every successful book launch is a dynamic team of designers and editors. How blessed am I to have my book designer, Melinda Martin, and my editor, Gail Fallen, share my heart and vision for this project. Their creativity and expertise brought it to heights I had not imagined. And, in the process, I have been blessed by their faith and friendship. You each have been a joy to work with. Thank you so much for turning a computer document into a gorgeous book.

From Will

I would like to thank Jesus Christ, whose steadfast love abided through all my folly and missteps, and to God, the Father, who through His loving providence provided a path for me, and to the Holy Spirit, whose whisper guided me through the journey.

I would like to thank my father and mother, without whom I would never have met Donna nor had the opportunity to share in her mission to touch the hearts of those who are hurting.

To my father, thank you for being a model of compassion and mercy throughout my life.

To my mother, words really escape all I have to say. You were vulnerable and courageous, suffering and gracious, terrified and faithful, helpless and more of a help to me than I could ever imagine. More than anything, you personified love. No pain, no illness, and not even death could take that from you. Your life inspires me to be a better Christian, a better husband, and a better father every day.

To my wife, Amber, I cannot thank you enough for the sacrifices you endured to make this project possible. You were a source of strength and support for me always, even as we were beginning our own family and I gave so many hours to writing and editing. You brought the greatest joys into my life: the day you married me and the day you brought Tripp, Bennett, and Luke into this world. You are the center of all that matters most to me on earth. I love you.

To Tripp, though you don't remember it, thank you for being my "writing partner," napping in the BabyBjörn® around my chest through many rounds of edits. To you, Bennett, and Luke, thank you for putting a smile on my face each day. I love you.

Finally, to all the people who have supported me through this journey, of whom there are too many to name, thank you. There are so many whose well-timed smile or kind word meant far more to me along the way than they'll ever know.

To all of you who have supported and encouraged me, thank you.

Notes

About the Cover

1. Jackie Carroll, "Propagating Magnolia Seeds: How to Grow a Magnolia Tree from Seed," Gardening Know How, https://www.gardeningknowhow.com/ornamental/trees/magnolia/propagating-magnolia-seeds.htm.

Chapter 5: A Year of Firsts

1. The author of "Footprints in the Sand" (and the date the poem was actually written) has been a source of major dispute for many years. Those who claim authorship include Margaret Powers (née Fishback), Carolyn Carty, and Mary Stevens.

Chapter 7: Going in Circles

1. C.S. Lewis, *A Grief Observed* (London: Faber and Faber, 1961), 10.

2. Harriet Sarnoff Schiff, *The Bereaved Parent* (New York: Penguin, 1978), 127.

3. James Robert Lowell, "After the Burial." See https://www.bartleby.com/248/356.html.

Chapter 8: Dark Night of the Soul

1. St. John of the Cross, "Dark Night of the Soul." Available at https://www.poetryfoundation.org/poems/157984/the-dark-night-of-the-soul.

2. Ibid.

3. Henri J. M. Nouwen, *The Wounded Healer* (New York: Knopf Doubleday, 1972), 4.

4. Attributed to Vittorio Altieri, an early 1900s entrepreneur.

Chapter 10: Two Steps Forward, One Step Back

1. Much of the content in this chapter is a synopsis of Dr. Elizabeth Kübler-Ross's weeklong "Life, Death, and Transition Workshop," which the author attended in January 1993.

2. Nicholas Wolterstorff, *Lament for a Son* (Grand Rapids: Eerdmans, 1987), 5–6.

Donna Berger

Donna Berger was married with three young children and was a practicing nurse anesthetist when she lost her family in a tragic accident. Since that day, God has taken her by the hand and led her to a new life, a new family, and a renewed purpose. She dedicates herself to helping others through grief, advocating for safer highways and witnessing to the faithfulness of God in her life.

Donna's blog and social media presence provide an oasis of rest and peace for those who are grieving. Donna and her husband, John, are the parents of three grown children and live in Florida with their dog, who is aptly named "Dog."

Connect with the Author

website	donnamarieberger.com
facebook	Donna M Berger
instagram	bergerdonnamarie
youtube.com	@donnamarieberger

Will Searcy

Will Searcy is a writer and producer who has written and/or produced over forty documentary films about individual injured victims' catastrophic loss. As an author, Will contributes to Donna's Christian blog while continuing to author faith-based works of his own. When not writing, Will serves in ministries through his church. He works in Catholic education as a marketing and communications professional and also has taught religion classes to middle school students.

Made in United States
North Haven, CT
07 February 2023